Normal Now

Only one truth appears before our eyes: wealth, fertility and sweet strength in all its insidious universality. In contrast, we are unaware of the prodigious machinery of the will to truth, with its vocation of exclusion.

Michel Foucault, 'The Orders of Discourse'

NORMAL NOW

Individualism as Conformity

Mark G. E. Kelly

polity

Copyright © Mark G. E. Kelly 2022

The right of Mark G. E. Kelly to be identified as Author of this Work has been asserted in accordance with the UK Copyright, Designs and Patents Act 1988.

First published in 2022 by Polity Press

Polity Press
65 Bridge Street
Cambridge CB2 1UR, UK

Polity Press
101 Station Landing
Suite 300
Medford, MA 02155, USA

All rights reserved. Except for the quotation of short passages for the purpose of criticism and review, no part of this publication may be reproduced, stored in a retrieval system or transmitted, in any form or by any means, electronic, mechanical, photocopying, recording or otherwise, without the prior permission of the publisher.

ISBN-13: 978-1-5095-5094-4
ISBN-13: 978-1-5095-5095-1(pb)

A catalogue record for this book is available from the British Library.

Library of Congress Control Number: 2021945288

Typeset in 11 on 13pt Sabon
by Fakenham Prepress Solutions, Fakenham, Norfolk NR21 8NL
Printed and bound in Great Britain by TJ Books Ltd, Padstow, Cornwall

The publisher has used its best endeavours to ensure that the URLs for external websites referred to in this book are correct and active at the time of going to press. However, the publisher has no responsibility for the websites and can make no guarantee that a site will remain live or that the content is or will remain appropriate.

Every effort has been made to trace all copyright holders, but if any have been overlooked the publisher will be pleased to include any necessary credits in any subsequent reprint or edition.

For further information on Polity, visit our website:
politybooks.com

Contents

Acknowledgements		vi
Preface		viii
1	Genealogy	1
2	New Norms	24
3	Politics	57
4	Sex	75
5	Life	106
6	Law	130
7	Difference	150
Conclusion		167
Notes		175
Index		190

Acknowledgements

I thank James Kent for his comments on an initial draft of this book (and for his broader willingness to act as a sounding board for my ideas), three anonymous reviewers for their comments and recommendations, and Robert Carson for his comments on the chapter on sex.

I thank my editor at Polity, Pascal Porcheron, for facilitating the publication of this work.

This work originates in the project, generously funded by the Australian Research Council as a Future Fellowship (Grant FT140101020), 'The invention of norms: understanding how ethics, law, and the life sciences connect to shape our social selves'. I would like to take this opportunity to express my gratitude to the ARC and to Australia more generally for this funding. I would also like to thank those who fostered this project: Alison Ross, who helped enormously with my application; Diego Bubbio, who also helped in this regard; Dimitris Vardoulakis, without whom I doubt it would ever have occurred to me to apply; Paul Patton, the relevant member of the ARC's College of Experts at the time the project was funded; the various anonymous

Acknowledgements

reviewers of my proposals for their feedback and generous estimation of its worthiness; and Adam Jasper Smith and the University of Technology, Sydney, for arranging library facilities for me while I was first writing the application. I would also like to thank those who hosted me on research visits during the fellowship, most particularly the Centre for Research in Modern European Philosophy at Kingston University London, and especially Peter Hallward for seminar questioning that forced me to add caveats that survive in this manuscript.

Preface

Am I normal?

Haven't we all asked this question at one time or another? Some of us might ask it frequently. The answers we come up with surely vary, even for the same person at different times. Some defensively assert that there is nothing wrong with them, and indeed that it is, perhaps, other people, the ones who appear normal, who are the real weirdos. Many of us concede that there is something wrong with us, and schedule an appointment with a professional in search of a solution.

What is at the heart of such worries? What are we trying to achieve by either accusing others of being abnormal or seeking to improve or cure ourselves? Of course, the precise answers are as many and varied as human psychology itself, but there are some general motives that most or perhaps even all of us have, such as wanting to be healthy and happy. These general human goals seem to me precisely to have become subsumed by a more general and distinctively modern drive to be normal. Happiness as we understand it today is our affective *norm*, as health is our medical one.

Preface

What is normality? Like many of the concepts in the cognitive background to our lives, it is not immediately easy for us to define. Indeed, I will argue that it is not a concept that has been defined adequately even by experts in fields that rely on it. Moreover, I will suggest that it is a peculiarly insidious concept in the way that it evades a simple definition.[1]

This is a book about what is considered normal today and about how our conception of normality has changed in a seismic shift that is still moving the ground beneath us. I will claim that normality has, in the course of the last century, gone from being a series of differentiated social standards applying to different categories of person to being a network of contradictory and paradoxical standards that apply increasingly indifferently to everyone. The pressure to be normal has always put people in an ultimately impossibly difficult position, but the new normality adds to this an expectation that we conform by refusing to conform, leading to the profoundly confused form of subjectivity we all today embody in various ways.

This mutation in normality is perhaps barely half a century old. The very concept of 'normality' in which it has occurred was itself invented perhaps only a few centuries ago. Although the word 'normal' is part of our everyday vocabulary today, it is a fairly recent addition to the English language (from French or Latin), only two hundred or so years old. Only about a hundred years ago did it become a widely used word. Its relative novelty does give us reason to suspect that our contemporary normality might itself soon disappear, though we can have little idea what might replace it or when.

* * *

Preface

Over the years that I have been developing the thoughts presented in this book, the concept of normality has proved to be a mobile target. First, around the election of Donald Trump to the US presidency in 2016, a prominent discourse appeared about Trump 'normalizing' adverse behaviour. More recently, in 2020, the arrival of the COVID-19 pandemic saw changes to people's lifestyles widely described as a 'new normal' (a phrase that was, prior to that year, the working title of this book, and which I abandoned to avoid this novel connotation).

Such invocations of the concept of normality, I would suggest, bear out my position that it is a central question in our society today. However, they invoke the concept in ways that are only obliquely related to how I discuss it here. The second chapter of this book does attend intensely to the Trump phenomenon, but I argue that he has actually normalized approximately nothing. I spend less time discussing COVID-19, partly because I think it is too early to draw any conclusions about its effects on norms, but also because I don't as yet see much evidence of novelty in this relation either. As I detail in the first chapter, recent changed expectations around hand-washing and social distancing, albeit constituting a major change to our lifestyles, is not technically a 'new normal' as I understand it, but rather a modulation of the old normal standards, harking back, indeed, to the very origins of normality as a phenomenon. Face masks and restrictions on movement are blunt measures, which we experience as oppressive, but there is nothing very new about authorities intervening to affect our behaviour in ways that are supposed to be for our own good. It is entirely possible that the current pandemic will change our society such that it will produce a sea change in our norms – but I

Preface

don't think anyone can yet claim to know this or what it might look like. What I detail here are changes that were well underway long before the pandemic hit, and which show no obvious sign of dissipating in the face of it.

1
Genealogy

In this chapter, I outline the history of normality, before moving on in the next chapter to detail the more recent development of what I call our 'new norms', and then, in the rest of the book, detailing how these have played out in different social realms.

I will throughout this book use the word 'norm' (and hence the derived adjectives 'normal' and 'normative') in a highly specific way, as I will now explain. This usage of the term derives from the work of two twentieth-century French philosophers, Georges Canguilhem and, following him, Michel Foucault. They in turn derive their use of the term 'norm' from the study of the actual history of norms.

This usage of the term then has a strong etymological basis, but there are manifold senses in which the term is used today that I am *not* employing here, even if these senses also do constitute part of the broad history of the use of the term that I am alluding to. I therefore do not use 'norm', as sociologists do, to mean any unwritten social convention. Nor do I use it to mean a formal rule or average; indeed, I precisely mean by norm that which is neither a formal rule nor an average.

Genealogy

My thesis here is *sui generis*, but might be said to intersect with (which is to say, potentially either dovetail with or conflict with) any number of other accounts about social and cultural change in the era under discussion. Christopher Lasch's *Culture of Narcissism* is a particularly clear example of a thesis that is in many respects close to mine, but which has significantly different coordinates and claims in others.[1] I have not sought to deal with any such intersections in any detail, however, in order instead to focus on honing my own thesis.

This is not merely a thesis about a change in norms in a sociological or moral sense, although I certainly do claim there is such a change. Rather, my conception of the 'norm' is much more specific, and hence so too are my claims. This serves as the fundamental point of difference between my thesis and a superficially similar survey of the sociology of morals under capitalism such as that by Luc Boltanski and Eve Chiapello.[2] This does not mean that what I say is meant to contradict such accounts. Rather, I would hope mine ultimately dovetails productively with others.[3]

What I mean by a norm is, in short, a model for the perfect operation of the thing to which it pertains.[4] I believe that this definition of the norm is the one with which Foucault and Canguilhem work, and which can be found in historical discourses about norms from the seventeenth century on. Other scholars disagree that this is Foucault's understanding of the norm, but this ultimately does not matter for the purposes of this book. Regardless of its provenance, this is what I mean in this book when I refer to the norm and derived terms.

Genealogy

Normality as Normative

Canguilhem's book, *The Normal and the Pathological*, written in the middle of the twentieth century, remains the landmark investigation into the concept of normality.[5] Canguilhem was a French medical doctor, historian and philosopher of science. His study concerns the technical question of medical normality. This ostensibly specialist work is more generally illuminating than one might imagine, not least because medicine has operated as a motor for the diffusion of the concept of normality throughout our culture.

Modern medicine is based on a notion of medical normality, which is to say on defining health as accordance with a predefined norm. Canguilhem's key question is that of the origin of this norm. Modern medicine clearly considers itself to be a scientific enterprise, based on empirical study and objective criteria. Its basic norms do not really measure up to this self-image, however.

Canguilhem notes that it is commonly believed in the medical profession that what is normal is simply what is average, such that the normal condition of health can be defined by observing what most people's condition is. He concludes, however, that medical normality cannot possibly be defined or derived in this way. To be normal is defined in medicine as being optimally healthy, and this is clearly *not* the average condition of human beings. Rather, most people are to some extent, in some way or other, *unhealthy*, which is to say that they deviate from the norm. Unless exactly as many people deviate in two opposite directions – for example, exactly as many people have high blood pressure as have low blood pressure, to the same extent – then the average will not be the norm. And such an absolutely symmetrical deviation in both directions from the norm never occurs in reality.

In fact, the word 'normal' only came to be associated with averages when statisticians in the late nineteenth century applied this word – which was by that time already in use in other technical fields, and in medicine in particular – to an extant statistical idea that they had called by other names previously, dubbing this now the 'normal distribution'.[6] However, I will argue that this invention of a statistical notion of the normal thenceforth serves to give a patina of objectivity to the concept of normality in general.

Canguilhem concludes that the medical notion of normality, although presented as an objective and scientific judgement, is in fact *normative*, which is to say, a judgement of what things *should* be like. Such normative judgements cannot be empirical inferences from scientific study – as Ian Hacking points out, statistical judgements of normality cannot have any normative implications[7] – but rather must be a priori principles. These principles are, in a word, norms, imaginary standards of perfection to which reality is held.

Although it might seem like a great scandal that medicine is based on prejudices, Canguilhem does not reject these norms. He is instead quite clear that modern medicine needs the yardstick of normality to operate. Discarding it would cost untold lives. He instead suggests reforming the standard of normality by abandoning the pretence that it is objective and acknowledging its subjectivity by making patients themselves the final arbiters of whether they actually are sick.

For my part, I am not advocating even this: unlike Canguilhem, I do not have a medical background, and am not directly concerned with medical norms. Rather,

Genealogy

I am concerned with what has happened as the notion of normality has exploded out of medicine and become a social phenomenon over the last two centuries.

Normalization

The concept of normality implies an underlying concept of the norm, the norm being the measure of what counts as normal. This is somewhat obscured in English by the fact that the word 'normal' is much more prominent than 'norm', perhaps because it came into our language first, only to be followed by the word 'norm' later.[8] It is the latter word that is older, however, in the tongues in which these terms originated, namely the Romance languages.

'Norm' comes from an old Latin word for a carpenter's rule, *norma*. For a long time in European languages, cognates of *norma* were synonymous with the cognates of a different Latin word with a similar literal meaning, *regula* (from which we get the English word 'rule', in all its senses). At a certain point, the meanings of these two terms diverged sharply. Canguilhem finds that this new sense of the cognates of 'norm' first appears in relation to seventeenth-century French 'normative grammar'.[9]

Michel Foucault, following in Canguilhem's footsteps, detects the logic of normality earlier than in the application of words derived from *norma* to describe it, namely in medieval practices for dealing with outbreaks of plague. While the exact point of origin of this logic might not be precisely locatable and matters little to the claims I want to make about contemporary society, it is at least somewhat important that this is a concept that has been invented at some point or other, and the fact that the genealogy of this notion involves plagues cannot but be interesting to us, living as we are through the COVID-19 pandemic.

Foucault finds that, in the Middle Ages, there was initially only one systematic method for dealing with contagious disease, namely that used to deal with leprosy: to remove the visibly sick from society in order to prevent the spread of disease.[10] This approach did not work with the Black Death pandemic that descended on Europe in the fourteenth century, however, because that new disease was so contagious that people spread it before they could be exiled. So a practice was adopted of continuously monitoring habitations once plague had appeared in a vicinity, looking for signs of infection and isolating any household in which it appeared. Though this was not exactly the twenty-first-century lockdown with contact tracing with which we are now so familiar, it nonetheless represents the same basic approach. This in effect requires norms – that is, specific ideas about exactly what a healthy person should be like in order to detect relatively small variations from these. This is still the basic approach we have taken today with COVID, where a cough or elevated temperature raises an alarm. Hence I do not see in our response to the contemporary pandemic a *new normal* strictly speaking, so much as an instantiation of an old one, albeit in an age of hand sanitizer and phone apps.

In contrast to age-old measures to control the spread of disease, normality has, in other areas, developed into something rather more sophisticated. A crucial development in this regard was certainly the explicit formulation of the concept of the norm as such. This occurred by the seventeenth century at the latest, with that notion and the derived one of normality expanding in influence rapidly throughout the nineteenth century. What is crucial to grasp about the novelty of this

Genealogy

notion is its original reference to an ideal model for the operation of a particular thing. Previously, there were perhaps some templates for making certain things, and plenty of rules – but nothing was governed by a positive model of perfection towards which a thing was pushed without ever entirely reaching it. With the introduction of the norm, however, increasingly many things began to be *normalized*, brought into a relation with a governing norm to which they were now made to tend.

This pervasive normalization began relatively modestly. French normative grammar was invented to provide a model to which people might conform in their writing, whereas earlier grammars had merely listed rules. Industrial and military norms followed as standardized production and regimented warfare developed in Europe, in answer to a prior situation in which incompatible components and motley troops were inhibiting the aims of industrialists and generals. The adoption of a normative model of the functioning of the human organism, not merely for triaging plague-afflicted habitations but for general use, in turn produced modern medicine as we know it, providing a clear standard to diagnose illness relative to the obscure conceptions of disease that had previously circulated. While we might certainly want to criticize all these developments – the suppression of natural change and diversity in language by normative grammar, the familiar woes of an industrialized society, the increase in deaths from warfare in the mechanical age and the mistreatment of many individual cases by a one-size-fits-all scientific medicine – we may nonetheless see this initial adoption of the concept of normality as clearly furthering the goals of the fields in which it made its mark.

After this point, certainly from the nineteenth century – and, I believe, accelerating more or less continuously thereafter – the phenomenon of the norm metastasized throughout society, a spread emblematized and perhaps even caused by the popularization of the notion of the 'normal' itself. Above all, two institutions are implicated in this spread of the norm.[11] The first is surely modern medicine: hospitals, and then the emergence of general practice medicine, spread medical ideas throughout society, dynamized in the twentieth century by the introduction of mass health insurance schemes (both public and private). Almost every individual in industrialized societies is now medically supervised – on an ever more continuous basis – from birth. Medical discourses and terms are increasingly absorbed and repeated by patients, used by them autonomously to describe themselves, and people start to self-diagnose based on medical principles without the direct intervention of the medical institution. A further, powerful mutation occurred via the development of a branch of medicine, psychiatry, concerned not with the body as such but with the mind.

The diffusion of norms involved a raft of other institutions, of course, and moreover much of this diffusion presumably occurred outside formal institutional settings. A crucial development, alluded to above, which occurred in medicine, but quickly spread across other institutions and then outside them, was the appearance of norms for human behaviour. Medicine's original norms applied to the organic condition of bodies, and norms had appeared governing the motions of bodies in particular situations (such as in military firing lines or on industrial production lines), but *behaviour* came to be medicalized and normalized as such with the invention of the medical discipline of psychiatry (which is approximately as old as modern medicine itself), and the later academic discourse of psychology (from the end of the nineteenth century). Psychology and psychiatry explicitly pertain to the human 'psyche', which is to say to our minds (or indeed our souls, to translate this Greek word a different way).[12] However, psychologists and psychiatrists cannot peer directly into our consciousnesses, even today. Rather, they must primarily be concerned to monitor our visible behaviour, whether or not they proclaim an explicitly 'behaviourist' orientation. All the new social institutions that emerged and became pervasive from the eighteenth century to the twentieth – principally the school, the hospital, the prison, the factory and, most obviously, the insane asylum – are shot through with this psychological normalization of behaviour.

Mass public education, appearing in earnest in the late nineteenth century, has been the other key institution for the diffusion of norms, besides medicine. For the first time, all children were required to attend schools. This new omni-education was intensely normalizing from its inception. Its teachers were trained in institutions then called 'normal schools', the chief function of which was explicitly to impart norms. The most obvious norms operative in schools are those of educational attainment, but mass education has also always been prominently concerned with inculcating more general norms of behaviour. These include the simple but highly transferable classroom norms of obedience and attentiveness, but also encompass a more general concern with the moral education of pupils: schools deliberately and loudly proclaim their mission to impart a broad spectrum of attitudinal and behavioural norms that are supposed to stand students in good stead in later life. Relatedly, the school is a major venue for the transmission of medical norms: morality and public health have always been normatively linked. This once meant that children's juvenile sexuality would be shaped and constricted; today, this approach has given way to an attempt positively to produce healthy sexual practices, as well as to inculcate acceptance of others' sexualities, but the basic principle remains the same, namely producing what is deemed hygienic and ethical adult behaviour.

What's in a Norm?

I imagine the reader might well ask, in relation to these claims of mine about norms, whether things weren't always like this: weren't there always such models? To this, I would suggest that we imagine this to be the case precisely because we are today so dominated by norms that it no longer seems conceivable that things could ever have been otherwise, or ever could be again. Although it does not affect the specific claims I will go on to make in this book, the critical force of my argument does depend to an extent on norms being an invention and hence being something that might reasonably be expected to disappear.

Norms in our society are different from the unspoken rules that also exist in other societies, in that norms are not rules in a strict sense at all, but ideals. What is different about our society is that we are expected not just to follow rules, but in addition to conform to innumerable images of how we should be.

This understanding of what a norm is, I believe, that which is operative in both Canguilhem and Foucault. However, neither of them cares explicitly to define this term, despite its crucialness, supplying clear definitions being considered somewhat gauche in twentieth-century

Genealogy

French philosophy. Foucault does, however, say the following:

> Normalization consists first of all in positing a model, an optimal model that is constructed in terms of a certain result, and the operation of ... normalization consists in trying to get people, movements, and actions to conform to this model, the normal being precisely that which can conform to this norm, and the abnormal that which is incapable of conforming to the norm. In other words, it is not the normal and the abnormal that is fundamental and primary in ... normalization, it is the norm. That is, there is an originally prescriptive character of the norm and the determination and the identification of the normal and the abnormal becomes possible in relation to this posited norm.[13]

Foucault contrasts the norm with the older model of the law, but I find it more instructive to contrast it with the *rule*, partly for etymological reasons and partly because of the greater generality of the concept (laws are effectively a particular kind of rule). The historical and anthropological records suggest that *rules* have existed in every human society, but are precisely not norms in the sense of regulative ideals. Rules are still with us today. Indeed, there has perhaps never been such a dense profusion of rules as we now have. The profusion of norms is, however, something distinct from this phenomenon, even if the two things are complexly interrelated and indeed compound one another (as I will detail in Chapter 6). There is a significant difference between *obeying* a rule and *conforming* to a norm, even if the two are often closely associated. This difference is the one between having to live according to a set of commandments and having to live up to an image of how a perfect person ought ideally to behave.

Incidentally, Christianity, I would argue, historically has been about laws rather than norms because, although it held Jesus up as an example to imitate, it also held that Jesus was God, and hence that, unlike Jesus, mortals are all sinners who could not actually achieve his perfection – at least not in this life. Even if Christ makes Christ-like behaviour possible through His influence, He remains an extrinsic principle in this process, always above and beyond. Thomas à Kempis's medieval classic, *De Imitatione Christi* (*The Imitation of Christ*), thus effectively contains a list of rules (alongside prayers and meditations) based on Christ's behaviour. The logic of the norm is diametrically opposite because it makes perfection *normal*, a default state that we ought always already to have achieved. This is similar to the Christian logic of implying that everyone has sins they should feel guilty about, but, unlike Christianity, it offers no forgiveness or sacrificial route to salvation, only an insistence that we should be without sin, something considered impossible in traditional Christianity.[14] In this way, I think the growth of the logic of the norm is closely tied to the decline of religion in Europe, though it also clearly relates to aspects of the Christian legacy and to the fact that Christianity has to some extent, at least in some expressions, come to conform to the logic of the norm. I will discuss this dynamic further in the next chapter.

To be sure, every society has had unstated rules of conduct alongside its explicitly stated codes, and sociologists today refer to these unstated rules as 'norms', but our society has a very different kind of unstated norm, and, unlike any other society, applies the word 'norm' to refer to it. Our society (which is to say, late modern

Genealogy

Western society), for this reason, can in history be classified uniquely as the *society of the norm*.

It is frequently difficult to be sure whether we are following all the rules, and even harder to be sure that no one will accuse us of breaking them, but it is possible, at least in principle, to avoid breaking any given rule. Generally, this can be accomplished negatively: while there are some laws that actively require me to perform some obligation, if I do nothing, I will, by and large, remain innocent before the law. By contrast, the norm is essentially positive, always prescribing that we should be something more than what we are (even if this implies the negative injunction that we stop doing or being anything that is not in line with this ideal).

This is not to say that the norm requires any *explicit* reference to perfection. Indeed, norms need not be explicit in any respect. Norms may be invisible and unremarked upon. Nonetheless, a norm always operates as an injunction for people to conform perfectly to it, even though this is always ultimately impossible.

One dimension of this impossibility is, typically, that norms are nebulous and phantasmic, such that we can never know to what extent we actually conform to them. But complete conformity is not even possible in those rare cases where norms are actually explicit and precisely quantified. Take, for example, the normal human body temperature of 37°C: if we actually coincide with this it is for a limited duration, and then only ever to the extent that the thermometer measuring us does not have the accuracy to measure our inevitable minute variation from this precise number.

I imagine readers might object that people have always desired perfect health, and so they have, but only inasmuch as they desired the negation of any specific malady from which they suffered. To desire to be free from sickness does not immediately imply a normative image of perfect health, even if the former paves the way for the latter. Now, there is a certain natural fact here, that we don't like being sick or acutely unhappy, but I am suggesting that the norms install in our minds a contingent goal of a total banishment of ill-functioning and ill-feeling. Such norms follow a widespread pattern by which norms are based on pre-existing imperatives, harnessing these and elevating them to unattainable heights. The norm of health may be specified in myriad different ways (and thus gives rise to many specific norms) in relation to particular indicators, organs, etc., but nonetheless implies a general aim of perfect healthiness towards which all such specifications are aimed.

Before the advent of the norm, medicine was negative, directed towards curing specific illnesses that presented themselves. Once there is a norm, however, we always vary from that ideal of health in some way. For most people, much of the time, this makes little practical difference: we still go to a doctor only when we feel sick, and the doctor tries to patch us up and send us on our way rather than chase some elusive ultimate normality. Normative medicine has the major benefit, moreover, that it plays a more active role in bringing illnesses to light, detecting problems earlier and identifying them more accurately. However, by the same token, the door has been decisively opened from the doctor's side to an interventionist form of medicine (with no ultimate end point) that means that, if they wish to, they can always find something wrong to try to cure, and to a concern on the patient's side that they are always to some extent in ill health, which is to say to hypochondriacal tendencies. Perhaps there have always been hypochondriacs, but medical norms allow a hypochondriac always to find some organic basis to point to as evidence that they really are sick.

New Norms

While our society is uniquely defined by the presence of norms, the specifics of these norms can vary greatly. We can presume that at any given time there must, in general, be only a single norm governing any given phenomenon, or else a major cleavage in relation to that phenomenon, as one finds in situations where organizations split around basic principles. I would suggest that multiple norms can only ever coexist where they apply to different domains, in different institutions, to different people, etc., such that within a given body of people there can only be one operative norm for any given attribute. We can, moreover, presume that there is a tendency for norms governing different phenomena at any given time to reconcile with one another, since, when norms come into conflict around marginal questions (that is, questions that marginally concern multiple norms), some kind of accommodation between these norms must be reached or else a social cleavage occur. Broadly speaking, if norms in different areas for people in the same group conflict with one another, there will be pressure for the norms to change so that there is no longer any conflict, or else some device for reconciling or mediating them must appear.

My suspicion is that our society is so normalizing that, in every area of our lives that we think about, without particularly meaning to, we posit norms and orient ourselves towards these. I cannot hope to prove this, and indeed there may be many areas of our lives that are not yet norm-governed. What I try to do in

Genealogy

the rest of this book is to show and discuss how norms have come to affect crucial major areas of our lives. My claim here is not that everything comes down to norms; it is, rather, that in our society norms affect everything, however subtly.

In the original expansion of norms across society, a network formed in which norms tended to accord with one another and hence mutually reinforce one another's demands for conformity. This produced a profoundly (although of course never completely) conformist society. This conformism reached its apex in the mid-twentieth century in Western societies.

It has subsequently mutated into something quite paradoxical, however. The engine of this mutation has been a revolt against conformism itself. This revolt occurred in part as a result of the importation of diverse influences from the rest of the world that called Western norms into question, in part through an uprising of people (particularly from the lower orders) who had never been entirely inculcated into the old reigning norms, and in part as a phenomenon of spontaneous reaction from within the normative order. The exact moment this revolt begins is difficult to discern. I would of course, from a Foucauldian perspective, say that there was always already resistance to the old normative order. The revolt clearly began to cohere, however, by the 1960s, out of more inchoate beginnings during the ultra-conformist 1950s, and reached its peak only in recent years during the twenty-first century, if indeed it has yet reached it.

Despite some more radical tendencies in such a direction, this revolt has not been against norms as such, but rather only against particular norms, or perhaps more broadly against a particular form of normalization. The overall form of the norm thus survived and colonized this revolt through the becoming-norm of the anticonformist ideal of the revolt itself. This produced our contemporary normative order. Unlike older norms, which simply demanded conformity, our norms today have been produced in line with new reigning meta-norms of *non*conformity and diversity. Where previously the only meta-norm was that one should conform with norms – which was hardly an additional norm at all, but rather simply an implication of the norms themselves as such – now the reigning meta-norm has become rejecting conformity with the old norms.

Norms are inherently conformist: the very existence of a norm as norm means that you are supposed to conform to it. The great contemporary normative paradox is that anticonformism has itself become a norm. This is the perverse result of a revolt against norms that did not overthrow the model of the norm but instead itself became normative. It is only in this era that something like a meta-norm emerges at all. Correlatively, the concept of the meta-norm is one that I am now coining to describe this formation; it is not something found in Foucault's or Canguilhem's thought.[15] And even this meta-norm only exists in a highly paradoxical form – namely, that there is now an overarching principle governing all norms which says that norms must be anticonformist; in other words, conformity with these norms must appear to be a form of rejection of another set of norms. Given its lack of positive content, it is hard to know what to call this new meta-norm. I will hence largely refer to it simply as our 'new norms' or 'new normal', but one might, for reasons I will canvass, also designate it 'radical individualism', 'hyperindividualism', 'postconformism', 'pseudo-anticonformism' or even 'hyperliberalism'.

Genealogy

Although the older conformism and the newer individualism are superficially opposites, there are deep continuities between them. They are united by a baseline demand for conformity to norms and also by a valorization of individuality, albeit that the explicit emphasis has shifted absolutely away from conformity towards individuality. Perhaps their most fundamental commonality is that they are both profoundly *essentialist*, but where the older conformism primarily enjoined people to conform to categorial essences, the newer individualism enjoins us each to conform to our own idiosyncratic individual essence. The earlier conformism involved different norms for people of different sexes and different classes, but enjoined certain norms, such as Christianity and heterosexuality, uniformly. A great shift then took place across the late twentieth century involving the explicit (but not ultimate) rejection of the ideas both that anyone should be treated differently to anyone else due to accidents of birth (which is to say that there cannot be any norm that treats some people as inherently abnormal), and that there is any norm that pertains uniformly to everyone. Every individual is now rather enjoined to express their individuality in whatever way seems appropriate to them, albeit within certain constitutive normative limits entailing respect for the individuality of others. The supposed abolition of conformism therefore established hedonistic individualism as our new meta-norm, because seeking individual self-satisfaction becomes the only possible goal.

Where once we were expected simply to obey the rules, we were then expected to conform to norms associated with our categorial natures, and now we are expected to discover our own nature and publicly confess and perform it. Where once we could rail against authority, then against conformity, we are now under an invisible

Genealogy

conformity that consists precisely in demanding that we reject the vestiges of an older conformity in the name of our own self-satisfaction. This new conformity is profoundly difficult to reject because it is so hard to identify, particularly if, in rejecting it, one does not want simply to reassert the now-vestigial older forms.

Method

In what follows, I will flesh out the claims I have just outlined by examining the way that these new norms shape our lives today in a series of different areas, all of which are enormously contentious. These areas and the norms that govern them are closely interlinked, and I do not mean to imply, by treating them under different headings, that they are somehow so neatly divided in reality. Rather, this is principally a device for managing the material in the book.

   I will aim here to be as objective as possible rather than being normative. I take it, following Foucault, that a critical understanding of norms cannot proceed by cleaving to existing norms but must do so by making some kind of effort to step outside them through objective analysis. In this respect, I am at odds with advocates of 'immanent critique', who think the best approach is to invoke some of our current norms against others.

   Despite my now denying it, however, I expect some will think that what I am doing here is condemning all the norms I describe and will then ask what alternative I am proposing, much as they have done in response to Foucault's critiques. While I certainly do have ideas in this regard, I have tried to put them aside. In many of the specific areas I will discuss, I think most readers will simply say that what I describe as the contemporary norm is the only appropriate way to behave. I can only sympathize with this view: since I am part of this normative order, it is difficult for me to imagine any other way of doing things myself. But the fact that it seems this way to us is, I think, simply part and parcel of our social norms being what they are. The norms that obtain in our society will *eo ipso* appear to be obvious and natural and right. The historical evidence, as presented in the following chapter, suggests, however, that our current norms are not very old, and hence we have no particular reason to expect they will be around for much longer.

Despite my aim of objective neutrality, however, in one key respect my method here will be highly subjective, since, on my conception, a norm is generally not a precisely measurable object. Since, on my account, no one ever actually accords with any given norm, quantitative empirical data is generally inapt to provide evidence of norms. What might count as evidence would not be studies of actual behaviour, then, but attitudinal surveys that show what most people think they *should* do, the kind of thing that is studied in the field of empirical ethics. However, on my account people are not even reliably consciously aware of norms – rather, the norm could be said to be largely unconscious. In Freudian terms, norms surely belong primarily to the superego, which implies that people who have them may or may not be conscious of them. This to some extent puts me in the psychoanalytic position of auto-analysis, trying to divine norms by analysing not only society around me, but also my own feelings and behaviour. Indeed, to an uncomfortable extent, this book might be said to be a critique of my own attitude to life over the past several decades.

Genealogy

While the subjectivity of my approach might lead me to idiosyncratic judgements, it is generally the case that, as a member of society, I should have as good an access to our norms as anyone, even if the mechanism of this awareness is rather obscure.

Of course, my perspective can be presumed to be different from others, in particular those who belong to (sub)cultural groups in which different norms are operative. This book is thus explicitly a study of 'Western' norms, and might be said to be more narrowly focused on Anglospheric ones (I am a British and Australian dual citizen) – which actually entails a focus on the United States of America qua the numerical mainstay and cultural centre of the Anglosphere.[16] There can be little doubt though that the United States constitutes a peerlessly influential and weighty example not only for the Anglosphere, but for the entire West and, indeed, to a lesser extent, for the entire world. Still, what I say here can be assumed to apply less to other parts of the West, and also may be presumed to apply less to immigrant and other minority groups in the Anglosphere than to the culture of white English-language speakers, the group to which I myself belong.[17] That noted, I am wary of claiming, for example, that this is specifically a study of 'White norms' or anything of that sort, so I will leave this boundary deliberately undefined rather than explicitly posit a dubious racial index in any given area. I thus do not claim that the norms I describe are exclusively 'White', but also acknowledge that I, as a white (and also male, etc.) researcher, am in a poor position to comment on the norms of others.

I must also acknowledge the variability of the use of the concepts that I place at the centre of my argument here. Like any word of natural, living language, the term 'normal' in particular is used in practice by different people in different ways. I do not claim that every person who uses the word means by it the same thing that I do here. In particular, people clearly do sometimes use the word 'normal' to mean 'average'. I am not saying that you should only use the word 'normal' in a certain way or that every use of the term is 'problematic'. I do however think that this word is the original name for a pervasive social tendency that I mean to critique, and that one of the problems with this pervasive concept is that it blurs the distinction between the average and the ideal. The phenomenon that I refer to with the word 'normal' is inherent in our society, a dynamic in the way we relate to one another and to ourselves. I certainly think this phenomenon has a close relation to the historical usage of the word, but in the end the name it goes by is not what is important.

Lastly, given that I have spent my academic career to date writing primarily on the thought of Michel Foucault, and given that Foucault is a privileged reference point in this book, readers might reasonably take the account I am presenting here to be a 'Foucauldian' one. I want then to hasten to clarify that this book is 'Foucauldian' only in the sense of being strongly influenced by certain particular arguments and aping certain forms of argumentation drawn from Foucault. While my debt to Foucault here is heavy, such that I could not possibly have reached my conclusions without his influence, I certainly do not contend that any of my own claims in this book were ever Foucault's (except in those cases where I explicitly report them as such). Clearly my claims here differ greatly from his. Even if this difference is at least partly attributable to the fact that I am dealing with cultural shifts that have occurred mostly in the period since Foucault's death in 1984, I also would not presume to claim that Foucault himself

Genealogy

would agree with anything I say here were he alive today. Nevertheless, I would want to suggest that, even if Foucault would not say exactly what I am arguing here, I am Foucauldian in a broad sense of following an eternal impulse to critique actuality, even if actuality at this point is marked culturally by a mutant reception of Foucault's thought.

2

New Norms

In this chapter, I will sketch the shift in our society's norms over the past half century, outlining briefly the normative system of the mid-twentieth century, before dealing in detail with the nature of the succeeding, contemporary normative order that has superseded it and examining how this supersession occurred.

Preliminarily, I will now re-present some of the core claims about norms in general just made in Chapter 1. I have claimed that norms lead to impossible demands for perfection. This unachievability of the norm has been greatly exacerbated by the appearance of the statistical concept of the norm in the late nineteenth century because this invention blurred the meaning of norms and normality, giving all norms and the notion of the normal the appearance of mathematical scientificity, even though in most cases there has been no statistical contribution to their development. This means that, paradoxically, the impossible visions of perfection that norms represent have come to be conceived of as average, which is to say not only demanded, but expected. Thus, even though all of us are to some extent abnormal in relation to the norm, we are all made to

New Norms

feel that being abnormal is not only non-ideal but also atypical.

A 2017 Yale University study of people's beliefs about what is 'normal' showed that these were 'part descriptive, part prescriptive'[1] – that is, a mix of a description of what they thought most people did with what they thought people should do. We want to be normal, imagine that most people are normal and feel ourselves intensely unusual in being abnormal as a result, when the plain fact is that everyone diverges from any given norm. We fail to recognize this fact and its inevitability, however, and consequently are trapped in a constant, doomed effort to be normal, which, far from making us normal, actually makes us deeply unhappy (a state that is itself categorized in our society as abnormal). Conversely, the difficulties that beset us, which for most of us are commonplace in our lives – sickness, to give a privileged example, but also bereavement, anxiety, professional and personal setbacks – despite being universal experiences, are never deemed 'normal'. Rather, we define them as abnormal, precisely because they do not conform to the way we think things ought to be.

The Old Norms

By the mid-twentieth century, for most people, the normative vision of perfection had become something like a vision of perfect averageness. Every American male – to give an example that is privileged in every sense – was expected to be the upright family man: married, God-fearing, employed, with children. Although the applicable norm here was, to be sure, an impossibly perfect version of this, which no real man actually reached and in relation to which every man thus felt inadequate, most ordinary men could at least meet its broad coordinates. Fifty years ago, if a man worked hard, provided for and raised a family, went to church, etc., that would be enough for him to feel at least basically respected by his peers and society at large. Of course, *broad* conformity was never quite enough: one was inevitably aware one did not entirely conform with the norm, hence life in this period was marked by the particular anxiety that nonconformity induces. Moreover, the norm of masculinity certainly did imply a constitutive exclusion of women, to whom a different set of norms applied, bidding them most obviously to bear and care for children and look after the home. While one can criticize this arrangement on the basis that the female norm was a lesser one, that to be a woman was in a sense to be marked as abnormal in a way that being a man was not, and also can criticize both male and female norms on the basis that they enjoined unequal power relations between the sexes, the female-specific norm was itself relatively straightforward to approximate in much the same way that the male one was. It is of course also clearly the case that a substantial minority of people, most obviously perhaps those who are same-sex attracted, had no appropriate norm with which they were even supposed to accord, but rather were simply defined *eo ipso* as abnormal, and had to effect to be something other than what they were if they wished to avoid legal and other forms of direct persecution.

 People today thus regard the norms of the mid-twentieth century with a mixture of nostalgia and horror. We are nostalgic for the certainties of that era, for its relative simplicity, but horrified by how restrictive it was. Indeed, its simplicity was achieved precisely through repressiveness (as well as, Foucault would remind us, by the active production of normal behaviour). Which aspects of that society horrify us tell us much about who we are today: our contemporary norms have been forged precisely in reaction and opposition to those old ones. We can suspect inversely that people of the mid-twentieth century would tend to have an exactly opposite horror if they could see the licence with which people now behave.[2]

The changes in norms over the past five decades are commonly viewed as the liberation of people from restrictive roles, and indeed restrictions have disappeared. It would be quite wrong, however, to imagine that this has freed us from the tyranny of norms. On the contrary, if anything, it is norms that have been freed to tyrannize us. This is not to say that we should (or can) go back. The old conformism was itself strongly normative and could moreover be blamed for producing our contemporary situation through the development of the norms that were already present in it.

It is hard to gauge when we reached peak conformism, in part because conformism was only ever one prominent tendency in our societies. Our society, however much it may have come to be focused on the norm, has indeed retained elements from its pre-norm past, and these offer some resources to resist norms. While we might think of pre-modern societies as peculiarly constrained in their thinking, intolerant and culturally impoverished compared to our liberal modernity, modern societies' self-image exaggerates their relative tolerance. Medieval Europe, for example, had all kinds of ways of accommodating those who would today be considered freaks and weirdos; while almost everyone then was obliged to belong to a single cult of a single religion, they found within it enormously varied expressions and lifestyles. In addition to the extraordinary forms of religious devotion that existed in that period, there was also the regular overturning of the established order in the carnival, as noted by Mikhail Bakhtin, as well as the de facto toleration of all kinds of behaviour at the wide geographical fringes of that society noted by Foucault, not to mention the survival of pagan superstitions in folk practices. Even in the age of conformism, residual traditional institutional frameworks allow exceptions to conformity, on the one hand (for example, it has remained possible for people to devote their lives to religion, even if some more mystical religious practices have disappeared or been suppressed), and, on the other, spaces of exception from the dominant norms have lingered, be they at society's geographical limit, or in internal spaces of libertinism and bohemianism.

Today, in a sense, bohemianism has gone from being a barely tolerated aberration to become the dominant culture, or at least what the dominant culture imagines itself to be, paradoxically making libertinism and bohemianism compulsory, which is to say, not genuinely libertine or bohemian at all. Indeed, what we see today is the disappearance of traditional frameworks of exception within our society canvassed in the foregoing paragraph, together with the normative colonization or appropriation of formerly exterior spaces. This has produced a society where almost everything appears to be a space of freedom, but which is actually more all-encompassing than any social form that has ever existed before.

Individualism

If there is a single fulcrum around which the late twentieth-century revolution in norms has turned, it is

New Norms

the norm of individualism, inasmuch as this is the most prominent single term in common between the old and the new normative orders. Individualism rose to prominence as a norm, particularly in America, in the early twentieth century. At that time and place, it took the form of a short-lived valorization of 'rugged individualism', and more broadly of the expectation that a man be self-sufficient.

The old, rugged individualism was a conformism of independence. Each man (for this norm applied primarily if not exclusively to men) was supposed to be sufficient unto himself, and the norms of society required him to demonstrate his absolute self-sufficiency as an uncomplaining father, provider and worker. This idealized self-sufficient individual was not supposed to be the author of his own values, however – if he was supposed to be autonomous in this regard, it was only in Immanuel Kant's sense, viz. that he was expected to arrive independently at the same universal values as everyone else, including a belief in rugged individualism itself.

Discontent with the Kantian universalist version of autonomy had been perceptible already in nineteenth-century thought, for example in the writings of Max Stirner and Friedrich Nietzsche, who articulated extreme forms of individualism, arguing that man needed to become the author of his own moral values, a line of thinking seminal to the 'existentialism' of the mid-twentieth century. However, the new individualism that has since emerged out of conformist individualism is not the absolute individualism advocated or gestured towards by the existentialists, but more or less its opposite. Contemporary individualism does not make us the autonomous authors of our own fate, but instead calls for each individual to truly express their innermost natures. Existentialism demanded that individuals take an absolute responsibility for all their decisions, something existentialists called 'authenticity'.[3] Today, what passes for authenticity is the supposed discovery of a pre-existing nature. In this way, contemporary individualism owes more to 'rugged' individualism than it does to existentialism. As I have already said, both viewpoints imply an essentialist understanding of human nature. The old rugged individualist was supposed to express his essence, but since only straight white men were truly individuals on this model, this singular masculine nature was the only allowable option. In the new individualism, each individual is understood to have their own idiosyncratic essence, which gives free rein to aspects of their personality in quite a different way from the valorization of 'ruggedness', and is thus to this extent anti-universalist.

The new individualism's norm amounts to the demand that we each need to 'be ourselves'. In a sense, rugged individualism told men to be themselves, too, but their 'selves' were predetermined according to a prevailing standard of masculinity. Now, the 'self' has become an open question, one we must answer for ourselves – but the answer is supposed to be a discovery, not a decision, which is what the existentialists had argued it must be. Being oneself today is imagined in terms of a defiance of any predetermination by anyone else of what one's self should be. However, this does not mean an existentialist refusal of any determination of the self as such. Rather, it means we are to discover a truth of our nature within ourselves. Quintessentially, being oneself today means pride in a minority sexuality or ethnicity or culture, but (as I will discuss at length in later chapters) emphatically cannot mean pride in the majority sexuality or culture, since this would imply adherence to the old predetermined versions of what the self should be. Those who are heterosexual, white, male, etc., must instead mine other aspects of their personality or preferences to find their unique identity. Thus, being oneself can be about defiant declarations of membership of once-maligned minority groups, but also, perhaps more frequently, an identification with relatively trivial personal preferences that differentiate us. The everyday implication of being oneself thus ends up being largely banal, a matter of following trivial whims, collecting records or Funko figurines, listening to particular bands or supporting a particular football team. Indeed, the struggle to normalize minority sexualities in particular precisely tends to reduce them to such trivial preferences: wanting to have sex with a person of the same sex increasingly figures as a personal preference in the same way that liking chocolate does. Contemporary individualism has ended up organizing identity around individuals' pleasure, by making the determination, nomination and realization of our innermost desires into the purpose of life. If what we desire turns out to be nothing more than having sex or playing video games, then it is these desiderata that come to define us.

The search for uniqueness largely terminates in trivialities because we are not and can never be as different from one another as we are normatively expected to be and because many of our personal characteristics are not considered suitable for identificatory purposes. Each of us of course does differ from every single other person.[4] We are, these days, taught from an early age that our uniqueness makes each of us special, but this conflates being exceptional in the normatively desirable sense of being better than others with being exceptional in the trivial sense of simply diverging from other people in small ways. Children's television teaches us that our individuality is precious, but some ways of being different are rewarded, while others are effectively punished. While native uniqueness is lauded in the stories we tell children today, various behaviours – meanness and violence prime among them – are clearly presented as undesirable, whereas others – traits like caringness and joie de vivre – are encouraged. Since violence and cruelty are ubiquitous in human beings and readily discernible in the behaviour of any small child, even as the child is being presented with an explicit message that they are already complete and perfect precisely in their own unique nature, their innate tendencies are being vilified as deeply flawed and evil. I do not mean by noting this to suggest that such instincts should be given free rein. Rather, my point is simply that the message of authentic self-expression is deeply self-contradictory insofar as we all have strong innate tendencies that are not considered normal (even though they are commonplace). The norm of authenticity thus requires a strenuous psychological denial of the very existence of innate tendencies in order to posit an impossible purity as normative, which is to say both as an average reality and as a possible goal. Cognitive dissonance in this regard is partially obviated by allowing that undesirable tendencies exist, but only as the result of undesirable and abnormal influences, such as bad media representations, or personal trauma or abuse, and thus can themselves be cured entirely through the normalization of all behaviour throughout society. This is not a new pattern in normative thinking, but where a century ago the aim was to root out the bad influences that fostered homosexuality, for example, today the aim is to remove the ones that foster homophobia. The specific ills we posit today have changed, but our general approach to curing them remains, namely that there is something fundamentally *unnatural* about abnormality as such and that it can be cured by restoring naturality.

This demand for the behavioural normalization of society to allow authenticity to manifest itself may be contrasted with older, more modest and realistic expectations that people should limit their behaviour *in spite of* their natural inclinations. The uniqueness of our society is not in telling people they are flawed and evil: in their traditional Christian mode, Western societies long told people *explicitly* that they are all flawed and given to evil. Our modern Western society is, on the contrary, marked by an opposite tendency of pretending that we are not inherently flawed at all. This, I think, is the fruit of a long resurgence of Pelagianism (that is, opposition to the doctrine of original sin) in modern Western thought since the Enlightenment.[5] Today, most of us scarcely think in terms of 'sin' per se at all, and have hence lost touch with the deep acknowledgement found in the doctrine of original sin (whatever else it might imply) that human beings are never perfect.

Norms in general do not accommodate lack (to which extent our era might indeed, as Foucault suggested, be considered Deleuzean).[6] The rugged individualist was supposed to be without lack insofar as he was self-sufficient: the world around him might be lacking, but he must meet that lack with diamond hardness. The normative revolution of the late twentieth century has seen a normalization not only of the individual but of the world around them, such that privation is no longer tolerated at all. The individual is never seen as inherently lacking, but only as different, and if the world around them fails to accommodate that difference the world is castigated. People are thus still expected to be perfect, but only relative to a perfect situation. If there is an imperfection in their context, this readily licenses imperfection in the individual, on the basis of trauma in particular. Since imperfection and trauma are ubiquitous, this significantly reduces the expectation on the individual, while producing new hyperbolic expectations of one's environment, including of other individuals. We have become much quicker to blame external factors, including other people for their imperfections, while being less apt to blame ourselves. However, the individual cannot entirely escape the anxiety of failing to live up to norms. Blaming others might deflect some of this anxiety, but ultimately no catharsis ever expunges its underlying cause.

The standard of normality has itself changed, moreover. The core normative demand on individuals now is to be happy, something that was not normative for the rugged individual. Indeed, the rugged individual was if anything expected to be above emotionality and affect, or, at least, the core of his individuality was supposed to be stoic enough to control and deal with such things. Such an individual might be understood as 'happy' in an Aristotelian sense,[7] but 'happiness' today is not generally understood in such an elevated or holistic way. Rather, it is understood as an affect. It is normative now to feel good, all the time, even if there is good reason to consider this impossible (how can one feel good without there being a contrasting feeling of badness at least some of the time?). Certainly it is profoundly unrealistic. Still, it is possible to assert the normality of complete happiness because there is always someone or something to blame when we do not find it. When I am unhappy, I can blame external factors. If someone else is unhappy, I can blame their inherent nature, claim that they are evil or mentally ill, etc.

New Norms

The old norms are condemned precisely by the new norms: they made people unhappy and prevented the expression of their idiosyncratic preferences. The very idea of duty, to which happiness was previously subordinated, is now denigrated as something that prevents the individual from realizing their true purpose. Delay and deferral in relation to our happiness are also no longer tolerated. Rather, the demand is for immediate satisfaction – which is to say, not just that we should be given what we want now, but that we should already have it, always already be satisfied and full and effectively without the lack that is implied by desire. It remains normal to desire, of course, but only – impossibly – things that we can already have. Desire is thus reduced to a matter of taste, hence a basis for an identity, devoid of passional danger. The demand for total satisfaction is impossible, but made relatively credible by its shallowness. Today, there is no distinction in the popular imagination between shallow pleasure and deep happiness, or between these things and satisfaction. What we desire is whatever we find pleasure in, and vice versa, and obtaining our desires and finding pleasure are together taken to amount to happiness.[8]

The new norm is thus a form of narcissistic hedonism. It is not complete selfishness, however, but premised rather on the ultimately incredible idea that the complete expression of each individual's desires will have both individually and socially beneficial consequences. Our hedonistic individualism thus means condemning traits where they are incompatible with the enjoyment of others. That is to say, it includes a liberal ethics that allows us only to enjoy what is, in principle, compatible with everyone else's enjoyment. What we see here, in effect, is the compresence of individualism and hedonism as coequal norms, such that they keep each other's excesses in check. The individual is considered utterly sovereign today, but is conceived of as constituted precisely by their desires and pleasures. In the old individualism, the norm was one of the individual as stoically resolute in the face of both external vicissitudes and the individual's own tastes and desires. Controlling one's appetites was, as in ancient Stoicism, a mark of strength of character. In the new individualism, however, individuality is defined in terms of the rejection of conformity to society's standards, the rejection of tradition and authority, in the name of following one's heart. Where this individualism is somewhat (although not entirely) normatively constrained is in relation to its self-destructive tendencies. Our era is hedonistic rather than selfish in that it valorizes pleasant experiences not individual tendencies towards ennui and melancholy. Of course, we are very familiar with subcultures that do valorize such tendencies, but these, I would suggest, remain resolutely abnormal – or rather, while the figure of the depressed and suicidal Goth is abnormal, the appropriation of the Goth look by brands like Hot Topic manages to turn this pose into a venue for fun (hence pleasure). Witness similarly the transformation of the old folk tradition of Hallowe'en into a night of fun, with once menacing symbols turned into cartoonish parody and ribaldry.

Hedonism, conversely, is constrained by individualism from the cruelty to which it otherwise might tend: if we did not value the individual as such, we might collectively seek to take pleasure in open bloodletting in the manner of the Roman circus. Still, this constraint of hedonism very much works within the logic of hedonism, once it is understood as a hedonism for all. Moreover, collective pleasure in cruelty is still licensed when it is directed at the enemies of our norms and in accordance with them, which is in no small part to say supposed enemies of our individuality and pleasure. It is thus perfectly acceptable to rejoice at the execution of foreign and domestic 'terrorists', for example.

This resultant situation, then, is one in which individualism constrains hedonism and vice versa, but where the two dangerously magnify one another where they are not in conflict. It is also one where there is no general acceptance of the idea that there might be any irresolvable conflict between individuality and pleasure. Expressing yourself is supposed to make you happy. Being happy is supposed to mean you are being yourself. The most we could perhaps acknowledge is that certain people's grumpiness is their personal form of happiness qua self-expression, which is to say that it is really a disguised expression of joy (which indeed it might be).

Thus certain forms of self-expression must be absolutely taboo. We paradoxically find ourselves in a situation where everyone is enjoined to be impossibly different from everyone else, while also being enjoined to curb that individuality to a degree that is itself impossible. All desires that do not fit into our liberal ethos are considered *eo ipso* abnormal, which is to say that they are deemed a priori not to be our authentic desires at all but, rather, aberrations due to the machinations of some or other unnatural and exterior evil that must in turn be excised.

Success

While contemporary individualism is based in the idea that we each have an inherent nature that we must express, the absolute valorization of this nature means that we do not posit any negative moment in it that might limit our potential. This is illogical inasmuch as any positive content implies determinate limits, but norms are premised on a denial of limitations to perfection. Normatively, a person's authentic nature is conceived of as a pure positivity without any accompanying negativity. In the absence of any tempering idea that human beings might be inherently limited, there has been an increasing tendency for each individual in our society to aspire literally to be the best person in the world, to be the richest and most successful – precisely as the authentic expression of their unlimited inherent human potential. I do not mean to dismiss outright the idea that human potential is unlimited, as suggested by, for example, Ludwig Feuerbach.[9] My point is rather to reject the inference from this premise to limitless *demands* on individuals, since these are manifestly impossible for anyone to achieve. Despite our culture's acute awareness and even celebration of the infinite differences that exist between individuals, the successful expression of our individuality uniformly normatively includes success by the quantitative measures of our society. We are expected to *monetize* our attributes effortlessly, monetization effectively becoming one dimension required for our self-expression to be 'full'. This is required because, in our society, we need money in order to fulfil our desires, and, ultimately, the limitlessness of those desires entails having unlimited funds. Since we cannot bear to defer the fulfilment of those desires, we demand naturally that they fund themselves. It is normal to be rich, abnormal to be poor.[10]

Of course, there are, to be sure, also significant countervailing tendencies, and there must be mechanisms for people to cope with the impossibility for most of them of even pretending – short of psychosis – that

New Norms

they are likely to actually become wealthy by monetizing their identity or become the best at anything. In the old normal, the inherent hyperbolic tendency of normalization towards enjoining each individual to be the best was checked by the fact that there were different norms applicable to people in different social positions, for the two sexes and for people of different social classes, in particular. These barriers between normalized categories have increasingly broken down, with normative differentiation pointedly rejected – not without justification – as discriminatory. Perhaps the sole group-based differentiation of norms that has strengthened rather than declined is that between those that apply to children and those that apply to adults.

One effect of this decline of normative differentiation is that poor and disadvantaged people generally find themselves under the same norms as the richest and most capable. While we might decry as snobbish (or classist, or racist, or ableist, etc.) the idea that different people are capable of different things, ignoring differences in capability in setting expectations is surely itself a form of iniquity. Our normative standards are strictly speaking impossible even for the most advantaged fully to reach, but the deficit is surely more glaring the less advantaged one is.

In the key arena in which most people generate their indices of material success – work – norms have changed substantially, such that pride in adequate performance (for example, in the length of an employee's service) has diminished, being replaced with a focus on exceptional performance and simply on becoming wealthy. Where formerly the overarching norm of work amounted to the performance of one's particular job, hence was indexed to specific expectations of particular employees, work has now become a repository of universally hyperbolic expectations that most occupations cannot realistically approach at all. Related here is the ballooning disparity in remuneration between ordinary workers and the highest earners: where once the reasonable wages of the middle class seemed respectable, they now seem pitiful compared to the earnings of executives and financiers. This is not merely a matter of appearance either, but is connected to a palpable immiseration of ordinary people, for example in major cities, in particular, where real estate prices are inflated to the point at which ordinary people's earnings become insufficient to afford respectable housing.

The new norm in relation to work thus denigrates ordinary employment. This norm is, namely, entrepreneurialism. This is a norm that ordinary people are encouraged to chase even while they remain in mundane employment. Almost any kind of small business can be reimagined as entrepreneurship, and even things that used to be simply ordinary jobs, like manual trades, are today typically the province of sole traders who have the official status of a small business rather than an employee, a process that has given rise to the 'gig economy'. Even salaried employees are increasingly encouraged to see themselves as 'entreployees', to view their paid work as akin to entrepreneurial activity.[11] This process of entrepreneurialization tends to reduce workers' actual pay and conditions, while holding out a possibility of enormous gains through a framework of employment that does not formally limit earning capacity.[12]

Even to the extent that people realize that such a prospect of becoming wealthy through their day-job is phantasmic, they nonetheless increasingly dream of making it big through some 'side hustle' or 'million-dollar idea' that they cultivate in addition to their regular work. Indeed, isn't the most common situation today for someone to be working in a job they do not derive satisfaction from, but with some idea that they will eventually either somehow strike it rich or at least be able to move into a career they do enjoy? The paradigmatic form of this in our time is the dream that a hobby will become a career, that one's photography or homemade jewellery or video game playing will make one rich. The norm that is now constantly invoked is that you should 'do what you love', which conversely effectively implies that the majority who do not love what they do are abnormal.

The full slogan is 'do what you love and you will never work a day in your life', a saying of unknown provenance that surfaced and quickly became popular in the 1980s, spuriously attributed thereafter to an array of influential individuals. There is a paradox in this slogan, inasmuch as it implicitly acknowledges the obvious fact that doing whatever one wants actually amounts to an outright negation of work. The hope is held out in this slogan that employment can be made frictionless, such that I will simply want to do what I have to do and never suffer drudgery, that I can thereby simultaneously work and not work, enjoy the benefits of working and the benefits of leisure. The cognitive gap here is closed by the extent to which people now hope to become so rich by doing what they love that they will simply be able to stop working completely and retire early. But the normative assertion that one should do what one loves covers an extraordinary gamut of scenarios, from the workaholism of the successful entrepreneur who genuinely seems to thrive on constant acquisitiveness to the indolence of a trust-fund baby, encompassing in between the elusive norm of the 'work–life balance'.

Boltanski and Chiapello note that, whereas the trend in management in the 1960s was to scrupulously separate work from the private sphere (thus avoiding corruption), the approach in the 1990s was to try to integrate work and employees' private lives (thus banishing the apparent deracinating drudgery of the workplace).[13] The consequence of the latter is, of course, that, while apparently making work more fun by making it more personal, it allowed work to bleed into and take over workers' private lives in a way that the restricted working hours of the twentieth century had essentially prevented.

Lurking behind all this is the idea that expressing our authentic self ought to lead to perfect happiness. The alternative is to imagine that achieving authentic self-expression is a struggle that might require us to give something up, but in the contemporary imagination any hardship is increasingly held to betoken a repression of authenticity that is simply unacceptable. While popular entertainment might tell stories about people who struggle to express their authenticity, one implicit message of such stories now is that society needs to be reformed to prevent them from recurring. This premise of course leads at its limit to the communist rejection of work itself as being too repressive in favour of a demand for immediate happiness without any form of effort.

American Christianity

How did we arrive at our radical individualism? The pre-existing norm of individualism is certainly one basis for the mutation of conformism into individualistic hedonism. Nonconformity can readily be presented as proving one's self-sufficiency: following society's standards might prove our ruggedness, but surely it is more rugged still to depart from those standards and strike out on our own. We might reference here the heroes of American Protestant culture, including Old Testament prophets, Jesus Christ himself, down to Martin Luther and the founders of various sects of later Protestantism, as well as the Founding Fathers of America: such men were deemed heroes by dint of their revolutionary rejection of basic religious and civic principles of the societies in which they had lived.

The emergence of radical individualism also surely had influences from outside the American Protestant *Leitkultur*, however, and was in part a reaction against it. Its birth can be located in the 1960s counterculture, itself deriving from the earlier American beatniks and before that Bohemians. That counterculture clearly defined itself in opposition to the dominant culture and had cosmopolitan influences (encompassing inter alia both Eastern mysticism and European socialism). Still, it was nonetheless part of the overall cultural formation of mid-century America. One might note, in this regard, that, though the 1960s counterculture contained elements of feminism, antiracism and (more ambiguously) tolerance of heterodox sexualities, by our contemporary standards it was white-dominated and rife with misogyny and homophobia.

The relationship between the mainstream of Middle American Christian culture and the American counterculture has been a complex one. There has never ceased to be a palpable confrontation between these two, but a countercultural sensibility has seeped into the core American culture to an ever-increasing extent, and thus into American Christianity itself. There has long been a liberal side to American Protestantism (specifically found in the Yankee version that had been politically abolitionist and, at a theological level, tended to bleed into outright Unitarianism) and this fused readily with the counterculture: major mainline Protestant denominations in the United States that did not already ordain women began to do so during the 1970s and these denominations more recently embraced gay marriage at approximately the same pace as American society at large, if not more quickly.[14] In this, a splintering of American Protestantism that dates at least as far back as its polarization over the issue of slavery has become more entrenched than ever, as relatively monolithic American culture at large has increasingly split into two camps, liberals and conservatives, with different values. Liberal Christians aligned with secular liberals more than with their notional coreligionists, as mainline Protestant denominations have declined numerically relative to more evangelical and socially conservative ones, leaving American liberalism increasingly secular.

More interesting than this dissolution of Christian social liberalism into secular social liberalism, it seems to me, is the way that new norms infiltrated Christian conservatism itself during this polarization. To be sure, the old cultural certainties did not vanish overnight, and the old norms have continued to operate among Christian conservatives far more than among urbane liberals. But the existence of an increasingly accepted and institutionalized alternative made those old norms ever more dubious, such that the decision to be a conservative quickly ceased to be a matter of simple conformity, and became a kind of countercultural position of its own. This paradoxical marginalization of the former *Leitkultur* allowed its scions to adopt some essential features of the counterculture they otherwise opposed.

New Norms

I might seem to focus unduly on Christianity in this book. In part, this focus does indicate some of my own preoccupations, but I think it is justified from a more neutral perspective by the fact that the society of norms has come into existence as both a replacement of and a mutation in a society that unambiguously had its moral underpinnings in Christianity. Christian social conservatism could be said to occupy the middle ground of American cultural life until relatively recently, even into the current millennium. However, its 'silent majority' constituency dwindled and became increasingly silent and decreasingly a majority, as it was subsumed beneath a louder avant-garde sensibility that predominated in America's coastal extremes and hence dominated its culture, notably cinema, television, publishing and music. With the increase of irreligion in the United States, particularly among the young, Christianity itself reached a point of relative decline where it came to be viewed by its more youthful adherents in particular as a stance of defiance in its own right, and increasingly embattled Christian elders ceased to assert the conventionality of Christianity but, rather, embraced a countercultural role. A concrete manifestation of this was the dramatic rise of Christian rock in the 1990s, to an apex in 1998 when Christian music comprised 6.3 per cent of all music sales in America, with Christianity deliberately draping itself in the garb of the counterculture, allied to the growth of charismatic Christianity with its rock stadium-like mega-churches and services that were closer in form to pop concerts than to conventional forms of worship. The justification for this, of course, was that such expressions are theologically neutral, but I think there is a very significant normative shift here towards understanding religion within a framework of individual self-expression in line with the aesthetics of rock music that is quite unlike older forms of religious expression rooted in corporate belonging and tradition.

At the same time that Evangelical Christianity was becoming increasingly countercultural, another trend, dating back at least to the 1980s but with deeper roots, was at work, namely the alignment of US Christian conservatives with capitalism. A key moment in this regard was the politicization of Evangelicals as a constituency in relation to Ronald Reagan's presidency. This saw conservative Christians at large inveigled into a 'small-government' conservatism via an appeal to their demands for religious freedom vis-à-vis an increasingly culturally liberal federal state, which made them backers of a neoliberal economics in an alliance with wealthy coastal social liberals in the Republican Party. This new alliance between Christianity and capitalism was not merely superficial, but skewed Christian belief, dovetailing with a recent theological trend on the increasingly charismatic right of American Christianity that has displaced traditional Christian opposition to materialism in favour of a so-called 'prosperity gospel' that promises material rewards from faith.[15]

Protestantism has thus tended either (on the liberal left) to adopt countercultural social values or (on the conservative right) to adapt itself to individualistic hedonism. There is today in the West a declining Protestantism of the left, associated in America with mainline Protestantism and in Northern Europe with national Protestant churches, which is relatively critical of capitalism, but stands in favour of the pursuit of individual lifestyle hedonism. There is also a relatively robust Protestantism of the right, associated with Pentecostalism and evangelicalism, largely emanating from the United States, that is relatively sympathetic to the pursuit of individualist hedonism through wealth and trappings, but remains relatively conservative in relation to sexuality in particular. That is not to say that there are not more traditional tendencies within Protestantism too, which remain significant, and I have said nothing of Catholicism and Orthodoxy. I mean only to note the extent to which Christianity has been blown in the wind of normative change.

Enjoy

Since the 1970s, then, the counterculture of the 1960s has blended into the formation of a new cultural establishment, albeit one that has existed alongside and in tension with the continuation of an older establishment that it has never entirely displaced and, indeed, that is presupposed by the new norm as the bad conformism that the new one enjoins us to defy. Still, for all the apparent tension, the conservative side has itself been normatively transformed. Over the past five decades, rebellion against conformity has become normatively hegemonic. This has been a gradual process and is perhaps one nearing its end: today's dominant, *soi-disant* 'diverse' culture can only operate by demonizing increasingly vestigial and marginal holdouts of more traditional, relatively monolithic culture and identity. It is greatly aided in this effort by a continuing hostile reaction to cultural change from these margins, even as that reaction increasingly positions itself as a form of countercultural rebellion. Should the new mainstream ever entirely replace the old conformism, it would have to modify itself into a quite different pose, one that is less rebellious and more authoritarian – indeed, we are perhaps already witnessing precisely this. To the extent that we are not – to the extent to which older norms continue to operate interpenetrated with the new ones – this is a peculiarly anxiety-inducing situation inasmuch as it means that everyone is exposed not only to one set of impossible-to-meet norms, but to two mutually contradictory sets of inherently impossible demands.

Two distinct normative principles at work today, authenticity and hedonism, might be separable in principle, but they are not currently distinguished in practice, and the current determinations of each imply the other. Contemporary authenticity amounts to an individualized hedonism. This individualization is mitigated only insofar as we can derive personal enjoyment from social activities. Individualism does not imply the total abandonment of the social precisely because the social is manifestly attractive to the individual (and because individualism itself is a socially constituted phenomenon), though it does imply some diminution of sociality due to the impossibility of finding complete social recognition of an idiosyncratic agenda. That is, other people will always appear as a hindrance to the purity of *my* enjoyment and *my* self-identity. I do not think it is contentious to say that, for younger generations today, engaging in even trivial social intercourse has become a matter of intense anxiety, and I think this is in part due to this effect.

People of course have always wanted to enjoy themselves, and there has always been some social encouragement of this enjoyment. But I don't think enjoyment became a *norm*, in the sense of a perfection we all strive towards, until circa the 1960s. Prior to this, enjoyment was, for the great majority of people, subordinated to – or at least shaped by – civic and religious duties. People have always sought pleasure and, by definition, seek to follow their desires, but historically

New Norms

rules and norms served to inhibit the outright pursuit of hedonism, always to some extent harnessing certain forms of enjoyment against others that are deemed dangerous. Indeed, this is still essentially the situation in relation to enjoyment: the difference now is that the restriction of enjoyment is generally presented as the protection of enjoyment, and the overt admission that desire needs to be curbed has receded from our culture. Our new norms are unique in seeking primarily to validate desire and pleasure; even if they often invalidate it, they pretend not to, which is the opposite of an historical situation in which rules and norms claimed to be against desire and pleasure but perhaps served them at some level. Desire and pleasure were previously powerful imperatives, but not norms as such.

When did enjoyment become a primary injunction? Jacques Lacan declared in his seminar in 1972 that the superego commands us to enjoy.[16] While Coca-Cola did not invoke the simple slogan 'Enjoy' until 1999, the company had used the injunction 'Enjoy thirst' in advertising as early as 1923. The brilliance of this latter formulation, which promises that the product turns privation into something enjoyable, is quite different from simply telling people to enjoy, however. Even recognizing the moment of privation that precedes enjoyment – a dialectical necessity acknowledged in Freud's position that *Lust* (pleasure) amounts to the relief of *Unlust* (displeasure) – is, I think, a step too far for our contemporary norms, or at least would today be a highly risky advertising strategy in light of them. Compare the campaign for the (admittedly much more obscure) Australian flavoured milk brand Oak under the slogan 'Kills Hungrythirsty Dead'.[17] While this is an extremely negative slogan, it promises as definitely as it can to negate the negation (the original negation being a conceptual doublet – a combination of hunger and thirst – coined by the advertisers). Indeed, advertisements in this campaign added further declarations as to what Oak would do to 'Hungrythirsty' (for example, 'burying it in the back yard' after killing it). That is, a negative moment is identified in these advertisements, but only on the basis that the product will completely nullify it, even though such claims are absolutely absurd: obviously these threats to 'Hungrythirsty' are metaphorical, but feelings of hunger and thirst are bound to recur regularly and can only be dealt with in a temporary way by the product, which is not at all analogous to killing them. By contrast, the idea of enjoying thirst is vastly more realistic: we will always get thirsty, but the presence of Coke will make that an opportunity for pleasure. Such an appeal perhaps suggests the beginnings of a kind of intolerance for privation that is not doubled by pleasure. We must suspect a deep source of this in capitalism, as revealed in advertising: privation is not a basis for selling people anything, so capitalism seems to propel us ever further towards promises of the absolute abolition of lack. Coca-Cola was born in the context of the temperance movement (indeed, tailing the temperance movement in Georgia by removing alcohol from his tonic to produce a 'temperance drink' was the step that led John Pemberton to first create 'Coca-Cola'), but as a result it actually subverted that movement, making temperance into a kind of alternative hedonism to the forlorn hedonism promised by alcohol. Thus we can say that Coca-Cola, both in its addictive substance and its corporate advertising, has propelled us apparently inexorably towards a pure injunction to enjoy – but it is only one factor. In the mid-twentieth century, post-temperance, it was certainly normal to enjoy oneself, but to do so only in a normal way, which at that time meant according to an image of propriety that seems risible today. Today, absolute enjoyment is a norm in its own right, against which everything else must ultimately be justified.

Universalization

Broadly, over the past half-century, our norms have become increasingly universal and unrestricted, while at the same time atomizing the individual. This seemingly contradictory movement occurs via the universalization of the norm of individuality itself. The old normative categorization of individuals by ethnicity, sex, class, etc. is now seen as restricting our individuality. Individuality is thus seen as something that requires liberation by the supersession of all normative categorization (although this also perversely today involves an attempt to destroy the old categories through a counter-categorization that asserts the importance of the old categories in order to elevate those in previously maligned ones and denigrate those belonging to heretofore privileged ones).

Formerly, people were united into groups by shared group norms, but the universalization of norms atomizes us by putting each person in competition with one another to achieve the same goals. Thus, rather than achieving equal respect for everyone, we have become a society that respects no one. Group norms were restrictive but also sheltering. By contrast, being free to 'be oneself' without categorical restrictions in the era of the norm does not mean absolute freedom to follow whatever path one chooses, but rather to follow essentially the same norms as everyone else, albeit in idiosyncratic ways – ways that are themselves

New Norms

predetermined by our individual natures. The very demand for idiosyncrasy is itself a universal normative demand that weighs on us.

Of course, some normative differences between groups do remain; different groups within our societies do have different (sub)cultural norms. Indeed, there has been a profusion of such subcultures in this period that sees a very wide divergence of norms at a superficial level, but I would contend that these norms are largely subnorms that point in the end towards the broader shared norms of our society.

Older differential norms do still linger on the margins, notably within conservative religious communities. However, even where they do continue to exist, the older conformist norms have to contend with a decline in the significance of the indices to which they apply, namely work, family and religion. While it remains normal to have a job, and while the norm of employment per se has expanded from men to all adults, the significance of work has declined. Previously, the unreachable norm of employment was the perfect performance of one's duties. Today, employment is approached less on its own terms than as a source of more general satisfaction. The norm of employment has thus ceased to be primarily devotion to set tasks (although performance of one's duties does in itself remain normative) and has become one of searching for the perfectly satisfying job. Family life has today similarly become relatively fluid, something to which we are devoted less for its own sake and more as a form of self-fulfilment or self-actualization. It is considered acceptable today to dissolve one family and start a new one in search of a more perfect match. The very notion of 'family' has become more elastic, definable in different ways to suit different individuals. Lastly, religion is in precipitous decline across the West, and has perhaps even come to be considered an abnormal commitment. For those who do tread a religious path, there is an increasing tendency to do so fluidly, by seeking a religion, or at least an expression of a given religion that is 'right for' us, rather than simply adhering to our cradle creed.[18] It is this and only this logic that can make religion normal today, when someone asserts that it is right for them as a particular individual without making any claim to the universal and exclusive truth of their religious beliefs, which in fact makes those beliefs quite unlike the religious beliefs held by most people a generation earlier. Conversely, the domain of leisure outside work, family and religion has increasingly moved from being a trivial supplementary activity to the core of people's identities.

So it remains normal to have a family, but the decline in the relative importance of this norm means that family life is accompanied by an increasingly unmanageable set of expectations extrinsic to it. Male or female (but especially in the latter case, given the continuing residual existence of some differential expectations – and indeed as-yet unavoidable physical realities – for women in relation to motherhood), we are today enjoined to 'have it all', which is to say be both maximally involved with our children and maximally successful at work (despite the clear tension between these objectives), while also pursuing identity-defining leisure activities in an untrammelled way. Though the traditional model of masculinity that obtained in the mid-twentieth century certainly licensed or forced men to be emotionally and physically distant from their families, it nonetheless was more realistic, inasmuch as paternal responsibility could be discharged almost entirely by working outside the home. Women were correlatively expected to perform all the domestic labour; expectations in this regard amounted to having children, training those children to behave within certain moral bounds, keeping a clean house and preparing meals. Today, while expectations of men to share in domestic labour lighten women's average relative load, women are now expected to do paid employment in addition to their domestic chores (while many women formerly had to work out of material necessity, this was deemed abnormal, adding shame to their overall burden, but also meaning there was no normative pressure for women to engage in paid employment where they did not want or need to do so). Women are also expected to engage in fulfilling leisure activities, while expectations on all parties around childrearing, in relation to education and children's mental and physical wellbeing, have expanded enormously, to the point, I suspect, that they have outstripped any additional contribution being made on average by fathers. One might think that children are the beneficiaries of this shift, but the expectations on parents to have perfect children are being passed onto the children themselves, who are now expected not merely to have good manners in public, but to be perfectly *happy* in themselves, a far less achievable goal and one that is more or less self-defeating once it is established as such. The new norms sweep away normative *constraints* on subjects, but increase the burden of normative *expectations*.

It is no longer enough simply to do what we are told, to like what everyone else likes: we are instead now expected to develop our own inclinations and individual tastes. The contemporary Western herd accepts members on condition that they appear to be individuals indifferent to it. We are thus enjoined to pretend that we don't care what others think precisely because others will think ill of us if they think we care about what they think. We are no longer forced to conform overtly, but are excluded in subtle and even invisible ways if we fail to conform to requirements that we might not know exist, and which it is impossible exactly to pin down. This is like a cruel trick, requiring us to behave in a certain way, without knowing what is expected of us, with the only explicit message being the ultimately disingenuous one that we are free to be ourselves.

In our new, unprecedentedly individualistic society, we are not enjoined to be 'ordinary' or 'average' but are, rather, all expected to exceed the average, despite the fact that this is by definition impossible for most to do. Yet, we are nonetheless paradoxically convinced that this unattainable perfect performance is 'normal' also in the sense that it is effectively commonly being attained – just not by me, or anyone that I know well enough to realize that they do not conform to it. We are contemptuous of ourselves and everyone we encounter for failing to live up to norms, all the more so because we understand these standards to be ones that large numbers of people attain.

This paradox can be seen in the fact that many people will happily insist that they 'don't want to be like everyone else', but to say 'I don't want to be normal' sounds nonsensical. We do today find people in certain internet subcultures, in particular, denigrating denizens of mainstream culture as 'normies'.[19] However, 'I am not a normie' is not the same as the statement that 'I am not normal', and the designation of others as 'normies' contains an ironic dimension that mocks the standard of normality by which the others are supposedly 'normal' – it does not necessarily actually imply that the 'normie' really is 'normal', and still less that someone who calls others 'normies' by extension considers themselves abnormal. Rather, this is a denigration of normality understood as average from the perspective of an elitist higher norm. Such a paradoxical denigration of the average is entirely typical of contemporary normality, even though it understands itself also to be average. That is, while we think of our norms as being met by most people, we are also acutely aware that we are surrounded by a mass of people who don't meet them, leading ultimately to an absolute contempt for this mass, since it seems to be incapable of attaining even the level that we simultaneously believe it has already attained.

I do not say that there are no longer ways in which we are expected to conform in a more old-fashioned sense: there are, and many of them. Rather, I am here identifying the trend that our society has followed for at least the past fifty years, and possibly longer, towards increasing individualism as the paradoxical core of its conformism. That is not to say that there are not contrary tendencies – indeed, there are movements, long present and growing today, that demand a return to a simpler conformism. No society is absolutely monolithic: all societies contain multiple tendencies that can point in quite contradictory directions.

3

Politics

Beginning with this chapter, the rest of the book consists of a series of four studies of different dimensions of contemporary society in relation to its new norms.

This chapter, on politics, will in large part rely on the discursive device of centring a figure who I think provides an unmatched normative barometer: Donald Trump. I choose such an arguably distasteful focus because I believe the political phenomenon of Trump has, since 2016, defined political discourse not only in his native United States, but throughout the Western world, and has done so precisely because of his ambivalent normative valency. That is to say that, in my view, Trump's success, such as it was, in rising to the US presidency corresponded to an extraordinary mixture of counter-normative poses and deep accordance with other prevailing norms. Perhaps even more telling is the reaction to Trump, which simultaneously combined a norm-driven hysteria that he might be 'normalizing' counter-normative behaviour simply by breaching certain norms with a forceful reassertion of what his opponents explicitly cognized as 'normality'.

Politics

The defenders of normalcy were right to see a kind of threat in Trump, but greatly exaggerated its extent. Trumpism has represented dissatisfaction with the prevailing norms, which might in this regard, as in others, justifiably be labelled 'populist', but paradoxically has remained in line with them at a fundamental level. Indeed, I think Trump's presidency has served to entrench precisely the norms that he violated.

Trump is an extreme instantiation of the duality of right-wing politics in our era, which is to say simultaneously posturing about some kind of return to traditional values, even as this pose in fact stands as a screen or even a vehicle for narcissistic hedonism, both in the man himself and in his supporters. For this reason, Trump constituted a very poor rallying point for anyone who seriously wanted to challenge norms as such; rather, his presidency saw the old norms slip further into obsolescence, while the new ones were affirmed more strongly than ever before.

Normalization

In 2016, the concept of 'normalization' suddenly came to prominence in the public discourse around Trump's presidential candidacy. He was accused of 'normalizing' a slew of behaviours that were previously not considered to be normal in the public sphere. The idea was that, by doing abnormal things in public, he would cause them to be considered normal. Pundits enjoined us to resist this and declare that his candidacy was 'not normal' – apparently on the basis that such declarations were a prophylactic against its putative creeping normalization. These calls continued during his presidency, with regular declarations that some new act or remark of his had further violated the norms of decency. There was a degree of cant in much of this discourse, with the notion of 'normality' deployed as a political weapon to claim that he was somehow utterly exceptional in his mendacity, when – as I have argued at length elsewhere[1] – much of what he did and represented was not new in American politics.

Trump did, however, flagrantly violate specific norms for the public conduct of American politicians in his language, as well as more universal contemporary behavioural norms in various regards. His extraordinary success, such as it was, I would argue was not coincidental in relation to this. Rather, people supported and related to him precisely as someone who appeared to be above or beyond certain contemporary norms, to shatter and break them. The Trump phenomenon at this point seems to have been – at least in part – a kind of failed revolt against aspects of the new normative order.

The prime complaint about Trump ended up being that his brash and boorish style violates the norms of political conduct: even where his policies were heavily criticized, this tended to be more a question of their presentation than of their substance. The norms of American political speech mandate a measured and conciliatory tone, the appearance of reasonableness and the avoidance of giving offence. Trump, by contrast, announced outrageous policies – such as a complete ban on Muslim immigration to the United States – that were clearly offensive to many and never stood any serious chance of being enacted.

The concern with 'normalization' in relation to Trump's behaviour seems to involve the premise that people's (or at least prominent public figures') behaviour generates norms, that norms trickle down from the top to the rest of society, despite the quite obvious differences between those that apply to politicians' speech and those of ordinary people. One instance of this concern is the notion of the so-called 'Overton window' of acceptable political discourse, and the concomitant idea that public advocacy of ideas 'shifts' this 'window'. Such concerns perhaps make sense if we think norms are averages, but, as I have argued, they are not: people behave abnormally all the time without changing the standard of normality, since everyone is always at some variance with it, and never in a way that is neatly balanced on either side of the norm.

The prevalent understanding of normalization is that it is a process by which things become 'accepted as normal'. This exact three-word phrase garners well over two million Google hits. It seems to have peaked in usage as early as the 1960s. In my view, this concept is oxymoronic inasmuch as no usage of the word 'normal' ordinarily describes acts that are merely accepted rather than being either average or actively encouraged. The paradox here is that in the society of the norm nothing is truly acceptable unless it is normal – that is, ultimately only the impossibly perfect is entirely acceptable. Acceptance is thus in fact synonymous with normality, but only because there is no such thing as mere acceptance in the society of the norm, since only the perfect could ever be fully accepted. This clearly implies that nothing actual can be considered acceptable where a relevant norm exists. This, I would suggest, is precisely why Trump's behaviour consistently provoked the histrionic reaction it did: if it is accepted, it must be normative.

The operative idea of 'accepting' something is important to consider here. To accept someone else's behaviour implies in practical terms tolerating it, which simply means allowing it to happen without registering a protest. Millions upon millions of people, all around

Politics

the world, witnessing Trump's behaviour on televisions or the internet, did not accept it and as such needed to publicly demonstrate their non-acceptance – anything else would constitute tacit acceptance of it. There were any number of ways to do this, including reacting to Facebook posts, voting for a different presidential candidate and, according to the newspaper's marketing, subscribing to the *New York Times*.

The entire logic of this reaction is ultimately facile, inasmuch as it requires us to perform non-acceptance as if what we are witnessing is a kind of witchcraft that, without explicit rejection, will possess our society. The very reaction indicated here moreover indicates there was no serious danger of Trump's behaviour being taken for normality. The normative stock of Trump's style has not changed as a result of his performing it in public. No imitators of Trump seem to have emerged, despite his evident (if inevitably limited) success. There is no evidence here, then, that a single person's violation of norms – even by so ostensibly influential a personage as the President of the United States of America – can change those norms.

How then do things become normative? Unfortunately, I think the short answer is that nobody knows, and I do not see any reason to believe that a general theory of norm-formation can be articulated (though I would of course welcome one if it could be produced). Rather, it seems to me, like so many social phenomena, to involve so many complex interactions that it can neither be predicted nor fully understood, only analysed once it exists, albeit in only an incomplete and partial way.

The quasi-statistical idea of the Overton window implies that there is a normal *range* of opinions in politics. I disagree that there is any such range. Like many areas of our life, contemporary politics seems to me to operate according to singular norms that organize it. Perhaps, in cases where there is genuine lack of consensus, there are two (or more) competing norms, one for each side of a debate. Acceptable opinions – either across the entire political field, or in specific political parties and camps – are nonetheless governed by norms with which one has to accord. One can disagree about particular points of policy by invoking more general consensus norms, including societally hegemonic norms such as 'democracy', or norms hegemonic on a particular side of politics, such as 'conservatism' or 'liberalism', for example. Of course, one can find people who reject all those norms, but the existence of marginal resisters is not evidence that the norms do not exist. Rather, exclusion from the public sphere of those who reject such basic values is evidence that these norms are powerful. No American politician could get away with condemning democracy as such, nor any Republican politician with condemning conservatism as such. Of course, a time can and probably will come when such norms will change and such things will be said. But this will not betoken a shift in the Overton window's aperture, but more likely (at least under current conditions) a sea change in our norms.

I would suggest that what might change norms would be the articulation of a new norm in a discourse that became widely accepted. This did not happen around Trump. Rather, the norms and discourses that seem to be more vibrant and successful today are precisely those by and with which Trump is condemned.

Trump as Abnormal

In one way, Trump's relative success seems to fly in the face of my thesis. How in the normalizing society can someone abnormal be so popular? One answer assuredly is that norms themselves, while popularly observed, are not necessarily popular in the sense of being popularly *liked*. Another answer is in the peculiar mix of abnormality and normality that Trump represented, allowing him to mobilize certain norms against others.

Trump is assuredly a very abnormal man in many ways. However, the features of his behaviour that were attacked most vociferously correspond to ways in which he is not very dissimilar to the average American: his way of speaking and his way of eating, both derided as unpresidential, are closer to those of ordinary people than to those of most politicians, using a more demotic vocabulary (short words) and consuming more ordinary fare (McDonald's hamburgers perhaps most notably, as well as carbonated beverages). Of course, one basis for the condemnation of Trump's behaviour is that different norms obtain for presidents than for common folk. However, the very existence of different norms of conduct for presidents and for other people seems anachronistic in an age in which, I am claiming, norms are increasingly universal. Indeed, although Trump is attacked for being unpresidential, specific examples of his conduct are typically attacked in absolute terms that indicate that his detractors would not consider them acceptable in anyone.

An extreme example of this was the episode during the 2016 presidential election campaign when a 2005 recording of Donald Trump was released that showed him making a series of allegedly abnormal remarks. One notable feature of his speech was its incredible crudity, his uses of the phrases 'I did try to fuck her' and 'Grab 'em by the pussy' in particular. The latter phrase was the basis of allegations that he had advocated nonconsensual sexual acts, that is, sexual assault. Tellingly, in relation to the shift of sexual norms over the past century (which I deal with in the next chapter), the fact that he had apparently with these remarks admitted to actively trying to commit adultery attracted almost no adverse comment.

In Trump's own immediate response to the release of the recording, he referred to his remarks as 'locker-room banter'. He thus himself effectively asserted that in public speech the norm is different from that which obtains in private conversations, specifically those between men in male-only settings. A number of prominent men then rushed to assert that, on the contrary, Trump's comments were not commonplace in locker rooms, though some other prominent men did concur that they were. It is not possible easily to establish who is right in this regard, not least because different men in different locker rooms might speak in quite different ways, and also because of a lack of reliable ethnographic research on this question.

The counterpoint made by most commentators, and by Trump himself in his ultimate apology, was effectively that his speech was not normal in the sense of not being ideal, regardless of whether it is commonplace. We see in this the decisively normative, rather than empirical, character of a norm. We also see the universality of the relevant norm: it was not accepted by any critic of Trump's speech, or by Trump himself, that speech of this kind is to be allowed from ordinary speakers but not from Trump. Rather, those things that he said that were deemed unsayable were deemed absolutely unsayable by anyone, in any context. This is, as I have argued, increasingly the general pattern of norms. Where once it was at least tacitly allowed that there were male-only and female-only spaces each with their own standards, today such exclusivity is seen as discriminatory and thus itself abnormal (as I will detail further in the next chapter).

That Trump said things that no one should say at all would seem to make him a fortiori inapt to be president. That he nonetheless became president, I would suggest points to a profound accuracy in his defence of his remark: while the locker room does not constitute a peculiar space in which norms are different, Trump's reference to it points to the fact that, in the real world, particularly in relatively private spaces, people breech the norms all the time – norms are at some point and to some extent broken by everyone in unguarded moments. This hardly means that everyone speaks in specifically the same way Trump did, but his defence does invite a general solidarity in the universal experience of being caught out saying the wrong thing.

While analysis has indicated that Trump's particular statements did damage his support on this occasion, in general I suspect that the abnormality of his rhetoric was a source of his popularity. I think most people would at least concede the general claim that Trump's status as a political 'outsider' in relation to career politicians endeared him to more people than it alienated. His abnormality is sympathetic precisely by dint of being relatively average or ordinary – whereas the career politician who approximates the norms of political conduct more closely seems, by contrast, relatively strange and even robotic to ordinary people.

Surely, though, isn't Trump, with his orange skin and eccentric hair, a bizarre figure? Of course, this is true in the specifics, but he achieves averageness in the directionality of his abnormalities. Take his sleep patterns. Trump sleeps abnormally little, 4–5 hours a night. But in such abnormality, he is not particularly unusual. The average Americans today sleeps only 6.8 hours, much less than is medically recommended – that is, they are already, on average, abnormal. Like Trump, 14 per cent of Americans sleep 5 hours or less a night – they are unusual, but still form part of the majority of Americans who sleep less than is deemed normal. Trump's diet is similarly clearly skewed outside normality in the same direction as that of the vast majority of Americans, featuring more meat and fast food than is recommended. Indeed, he is also, like most Americans, clearly overweight. Because he is abnormal in the same general direction that ordinary Americans are abnormal, they can see him as an avatar of their urge to resist the contemporary norms that they feel are imposed upon them.

There was a trend on Twitter in 2018 to describe the everyday self-reported activities of one's political opponents ironically as 'normal' (specifically using phrases such as 'having a normal one'), thus highlighting, as a form of critique, the strangeness of their life patterns. This seemed to originate in criticism of the Trump administration, but it was extraordinarily fecund – and ultimately futile – because anyone's everyday behaviour when subjected to scrutiny can readily be described as abnormal. After all, what can, without irony, really be described as totally normal? Some basic functions might in the most general case be described as normal: eating, breathing and sleeping, for example. When we start focusing on *what* someone eats, or *when* they sleep, or indeed even the way and what they breathe, things get murkier. Perhaps it could be said to be normal to go to bed at 11pm, sleep for eight hours, and wake at 7am. However, if someone did this punctually every day without fail, wouldn't this absolute regularity be considered abnormal in itself? Such regularity deviates from what the average person does, certainly, but I'd suggest that it isn't considered ideal behaviour either. It is, rather, considered normal to live a somewhat varied lifestyle, to sometimes stay up late or sleep late as circumstances require or allow. Our normative ideal in relation to sleep, I would suggest, is not even internally coherent: while it is clearly considered ideal to be always sufficiently rested, the ideal person would also have the capacity to stay up late and wake early as required; they would be the life of the party, having no difficulty or flagging energy at night, while also being able to rise at dawn to exercise, managing their full workload. In other words, it is considered normal both to stay up late and to get up early, but not to feel tired during the day, even though someone who managed to survive on very little sleep with no ill effects would clearly be abnormal. We are dealing here with the interaction of at least two competing norms, of health and of hedonism, a duality that I will consider in more detail in Chapter 5. Such normative demands are surely contributing to what is, by the norms of medicine, a recognized epidemic of sleeplessness today. I would suggest that this is due to the disappearance of constraining normative expectations around night-time activity that, even if they made insomniacs and *bons vivants* feel abnormal, at least ensured that people were not overburdened with expectations to stay awake.

The anti-Trump 'resistance' insistently asserted against Trump's presidency that 'this is not normal'. But the actual is never normal. It never accords with the norms that obtain within it. It is hence always possible to posit a crisis.

In the condemnation of Trump's more personal behaviour, the operative norm would seem to be an ideal of entirely inoffensive speech and conduct, which is surely as unattainable as any norm, inasmuch as there is simply no speech or conduct that can be guaranteed to offend no one. The impossibility of meeting this goal is one reason that the rules of political correctness are constantly shifting: they have to keep changing as it becomes clear that any actual speech continues to offend some people.

An extraordinary recent study showed that political correctness tracked primarily to levels of education and was opposed by a massive majority of Americans of every ethnicity.[2] However, the fact that most people do not concur with something does not prevent it from operating as a norm that everyone feels they must obey. The majority of Americans who find political correctness cloying nonetheless feel bound by its strictures (indeed, this is precisely what they don't like about it), even though it has no official force and no genuine consensus behind it – even those who pointedly refuse to do what is politically correct acknowledge the force of the norm and react against it. And to cast a secret ballot for a deliberately politically incorrect presidential candidate is something they can do without formally violating that norm, since it is, strictly speaking, a norm that applies only to pronouncements that are heard by others.

I think it is not coincidental that a lack of formal education is a major indicator of someone's likelihood to vote for Trump.[3] The more educated are *eo ipso* more heavily normalized than the less educated.

Trump as Normal

Of course, the natural response to my claim that Trump is some kind of everyman is to point out that, as a very wealthy media star, he is anything but ordinary. One might even say that, in these respects, he is not *normal*, but, by the concept of normality I am invoking here, he *is* normal in the ways in which he is exceptional. He is normal in the sense that he embodies an ideal, namely his crass combination of low-brow appetites and ostentatious displays of wealth. One circulating rhetorical trope accurately notes that Trump is 'a poor guy's idea of a rich guy'. Given that being rich is now a general norm to which everyone aspires, Trump is something of a role model for many people: he is famous, apparently powerful, apparently rich, apparently healthy, and he enjoys himself in a way that most people understand and aspire to. His presidency is a symptom of what has happened to the American working class, in that his election represents an age in which respect accrues only to the wealthy, in which being wealthy has become a necessary prerequisite for deeming one's life a success (think of Trump's frequent characterization of his opponents as 'losers'), making self-respect for ordinary workers nigh-on unachievable. The shift to this new normal can be associated with widespread support for a 'maximax' economics, whereby people of modest means are willing to support policies that benefit the wealthy. This is in no small part because people identify not with their actual situation, but with the one they aspire to, which is to say what they consider normal – being wealthy.

Trump is like and unlike American workers in exactly the right ways to garner support from a certain section of them. He seems to be one of them in many ways: he is portly, eats hamburgers, has culturally low tastes more generally, speaks crudely and imprecisely, but also seems to have a perfect lifestyle, replete with luxury and leisure, and claims to be perfectly healthy. Almost all of this offends more upper-middle-class sensibilities. This is not because the educated middle class has substantially different norms, but because Trump's abnormalities are ones that middle-class people manage to avoid more than he does. This makes him seem pathetic in their eyes, while his ability to attain the norms (particularly wealth and power) that the *hauts bourgeois* also aspire to makes them resent him for achieving such things without achieving their level of cultivation. College-educated people might sniff at the fact that Trump has an Ivy League education while being apparently dumber than them, but to the working class this combination of prestigious testamur with a lack of cultural elevation tends simply to be impressive. This is less a matter of different norms obtaining for different classes as of people from different classes having different relations to realizing the same norms. The middle-class person hopes to become wealthy, but by merit and hard work; the working-class person is more likely to hope to become wealthy simply by winning the lottery, and thus can respect Trump for the extent to which he became wealthy through luck and even (alleged) criminality.

Political Ideology as Norm

Of course, it is not only Trump's personality and speech that are held to be abnormal; his political positions, too, are held to be dangerously aberrant, 'normalizing' extreme ideas. At a policy level, however, I think there was really nothing drastically abnormal about Trump. Abnormal enough perhaps that much of the American establishment coalesced against him, but not so abnormal that they decisively acted to prevent or prematurely end his presidency, motions to impeach him meaning little when they were not backed by sufficient congressional numbers to be enforced.

What are the political norms today? A particularly hegemonic one, perhaps the most pernicious of our time, one that threatens to doom us all, is that economic growth is good. In this there is no optimal level; rather, more growth is considered better with no upper limit. No major politician seriously challenges this norm: certainly not Trump, but also not even Bernie Sanders, who might be said to be his equivalent on the left, at least within the context of the 2016 and 2020 Democratic primary contests.

Trump and Sanders have, however, both consistently challenged the related economic norm of free trade, the ideal of an economy without barriers. This utopianism of free trade has never enjoyed societal consensus, but such a norm doesn't need to operate strongly in the imaginations of ordinary people, only policymakers and captains of industry. Trump, by contrast, was only ever a minor capitalist, and understood international interactions as a form of competition, with nations understood on the model of companies, hence applied a quite different norm to trade deals. This is not a novel idea – in fact, it's rather an old one. Trump's agnosticism towards free trade was one of his less controversial opinions, because it served a stronger norm, namely the United States' self-interest. The supervening force of norms involving US national economic and security interests meant that Trump's protectionist bent could find purchase within the existing normative structure: when he declared a trade war with China, this effort dovetailed with national security hawkishness and thus did not face overwhelming opposition from the political establishment.

Such specific politico-economic norms are only contingently related to the governing norms of our contemporary individualism, although there is clearly some organic connection between them insofar as neoliberalism's deification of the market interlocks with norms that enjoin unlimited economic acquisitiveness and sanctify the individual.

On the economic axis, left–right differences today are less about normative goals than about whether to apportion blame for failing to be happy to the individual or their environment. The left archetypically holds that problems in individuals are not innate; deep-seated personality disorders, for example, are held to result from environmental circumstances. Problems can be acknowledged to be inherent (for example, genetic) only to the extent that they are seen as remediable by environmental fixes. The right also holds that individuals' problems are not innate, but, rather, that the individual fails morally in not doing what is required of them within an environment that is relatively benign. The left does not hold that there is no such thing as a moral failing, but tends nowadays to see moral failings as essentially applicable only in situations where an individual is relatively 'privileged' and therefore does not have an adequate environmental excuse. The right, correlatively, can accept that there are failures that are environmental in aetiology, but only when those failures affect people whom the right sees as clearly morally deserving of them.

The new norms are found in their least alloyed form on the political 'left', or more precisely among the socially progressive. The new norms can be connected through the rejection of lack to a more traditional economic leftism (that is, to socialism), but in their current form are specific to the present moment, which is economically right (specifically neoliberal) and socially left-liberal. Cultural conservatism, by contrast, today constitutes a varied mixture of pre-normative cultural relicts, older norms remaining in circulation and the new norms themselves. These exist sometimes separately from, sometimes mixed together with, and sometimes hybridized with one another.

Trump represented a peculiar form of the general pattern of contemporary conservatism, as a culture war avatar for a faction of reactionaries who want to pursue their narcissistic hedonism in a framework of quasi-traditional values. Trumpism was, and still is, precisely a revolt against new norms, ambiguously on behalf of older norms. Though much of his support and rhetoric does hearken back to such norms, his behaviour is in no way reminiscent of anything that had gone before. It is therefore scarcely credible that nostalgia for older norms is the main motive for his supporters so much as hostility towards the new ones – it was this hostility to changes in contemporary America, not only cultural but also economic, that provided the negative basis of his electoral support. In this, his victory resembles, in an inverted way, Barrack Obama's 2008 victorious campaign for 'change'. This, after all, could mean all things to all people – only those who strongly fear change would oppose it. In the same way, Trump's slogan 'Make America Great Again' is powerfully ambiguous inasmuch as it is not exactly clear when America was previously supposed to have been great. While Trump clearly had supporters who imagined this as meaning the old-normal social conservatism of the 1950s, I would suggest that the more prevalent interpretation was actually to mean some point in the 1980s or 1990s. Trump himself was a figure from the popular culture of that era. Neither he nor many of his supporters are so conservative that they would want to go back to a

Politics

period before the new norms. They rather preferred an earlier expression of the new norms wherein they were balanced by the old ones and were thus not so dominant.

4

Sex

This chapter deals with norms in relation to sex in both its major senses, which is to say, in relation to sexuality and in relation to what today is more usually called 'gender'. As I will argue, norms in relation to these two areas are significantly linked. They derive from more general features of our new normal, namely the determination of the meaning of life as satisfying our desires and the absolute sovereignty of the individual in determining the truth of their essential desires as the basis of their identity as an individual. This leads in fact to a situation in which personal identity is grounded in naturalistic hedonism, which in turn is largely phantasmic, inasmuch as people's understanding of their own inclinations is necessarily mediated by their socially constituted imaginaries.

Sexuality

Human sexuality provides the most glaring example of the shift in what has been considered normal over the past half century in the West. Not so long ago

– as recently as sixty years ago in America – being homosexual was not only considered abnormal by most people, but constituted something like the archetype of abnormality. Homosexual acts were prosecutable crimes in most of the West and homosexual inclinations were classified as a mental disorder. The old norm of sexuality in relation to which homosexuality was deemed entirely abnormal was one of heterosexual monogamy. Heterosexuality outside marriage was more tolerated than homosexuality was, and since marriage by definition described only heterosexual relationships, homosexuality was *eo ipso* both extra-marital and abnormal. For the unmarried (albeit that remaining unmarried well into adulthood was generally considered abnormal in itself), a norm of celibacy applied, but in this era of differential norms this applied much more strongly to women than to men.

The struggle for gay liberation can be thought of as a struggle for same-sex attraction and relationships to be considered just as normal as heterosexuality. This goal still remains to be fully achieved, but is nonetheless palpably close, at least insofar as this principle is now publicly assented to by a clear majority and enshrined in law in most if not all of the West. If non-heterosexual inclinations have not yet been fully normalized, I would suggest that this is because the older norms continue to circulate alongside the new ones. The prevailing norms, however, are themselves neutral in relation to the gender orientation of sexual attraction.

What does it mean, though, for two opposite sexual orientations, heterosexuality and homosexuality, to be considered equally normal? Does it not mean there must be not one new norm of sexuality, but two coequal sexual norms? Indeed, since other sexualities, most obviously bisexuality, but increasingly a host of other possibilities, are also considered normal by the same token that homosexuality is, would this not imply an indefinite profusion of such norms? The short answer to this question is 'yes', insofar as each sexuality may itself be norm-governed. However, all such norms qua norms encounter the same basic problem that no human being's innate sexuality will ever be perfectly in accordance with any of them. Neither 'homosexuality' nor 'heterosexuality' will ever perfectly describe the entirety of any individual's sexual inclinations. Moreover, attraction is itself ambiguous. What ultimately constitutes 'sexual attraction'? There are surely occasions where there can scarcely be any doubt, but there will always be plenty of marginal cases.

Of course, such difficulties are dealt with in the contemporary discourse around sexuality by, on the one hand, allowing that being heterosexual does not necessarily mean that one *never* feels any attraction to members of one's own sex, but, rather, suggests a durable and overwhelming tendency to attraction to the opposite sex, and, on the other hand, allowing that there is an indefinite spectrum of sexuality. Indeed, the contemporary understanding tends to be that the formal measure of a person's sexuality must be their self-reported identification. Publicly, the principle operates that we must take people's self-reports at face value: openly questioning anyone's self-reported sexuality is taboo. This is not to say that there is not endless whispered speculation about people's sexuality. This is bound to persist because self-reported identifications are never final: no one is too old to come out, or indeed conversely to repudiate their homosexuality. Self-reported identifications are thus always suspect. Nonetheless, the operative norm is that everyone will ultimately realize what their sexuality is and report it accurately.

The ambiguity of sexual inclinations coupled with this norm of self-definition pushes people always to further specify their sexualities in a way that more accurately fits with the complexity of their inclinations. This most obviously and commonly means identifying as bisexual – but the idea of perfect equanimity in attraction to the two sexes is perhaps even less likely to obtain than exclusive attraction to people of one sex, hence the ongoing profusion of novel sexual categorizations. The difficulty of fitting with these norms can be presumed to drive the proliferation of sexualities as people seek norms that better fit their inherently ambiguous sexual orientation.

Any difficulty in defining one's sexuality today is, however, rendered relatively trivial by the extent to which the question of the gender of the object of one's sexual affection has simply ceased to be normative. Indeed, this is a case of a much broader move – which I will discuss further below – to disqualify gender itself as a normative consideration *tout court*. Gender remains the single variable in relation to which sexuality is most classified, but to this extent one's sexuality has ceased to be a question of normality. The norms that govern sexualities are classificatory, but for the most part that classification itself is not about being abnormal or normal. So, for example, one will be thought of as an abnormal heterosexual if one doesn't meet the norm of heterosexuality, but being heterosexual is itself no longer considered particularly normal, so the only consequence of failing to meet the norms of heterosexuality is having to contend with an expectation that one should reclassify one's sexuality.

There is a single norm that governs sexual behaviour in general today, and that still does result in certain sexual orientations being considered generically abnormal, but it is quite a different one from that which previously obtained in this sphere. Formerly, what was considered normal was to couple with someone of the opposite sex, in a monogamous marriage, and to have children together. Today, what has come to be the norm in sexuality is the expression of one's innate orientation. The determinant of whether sexual desire is normal is thus whether sex is desired. Sexual intercourse is therefore deemed normal when it accords with the desire of all parties involved. The determinant of normality now becomes absolute *consent* in sexual intercourse, as the standard that any acts are in accordance with the desires of all involved parties.

Consent is not an entirely new consideration in relation to sex – it has long been a consideration in jurisprudence – but it has never previously had the same prominence as a principle against which sex is to be judged. Today, increasingly, the sole normative question asked about sex is whether it is consensual. The question of authenticity is not apt to be the object of the same kind of normative focus because, in the end, if someone says that they are being authentic we have little basis on which to disagree. Concerns about authenticity therefore themselves devolve on questions of consent. We are not expected to be concerned with whether or not a sexual partner's proclaimed desire is authentic, because the authority to decide that is ascribed to the individual themselves alone.

The effective corollary of the normalization of same-sex attraction has been the radical abnormalization of nonconsensual sexual relations. One token of how complete this shift has been is that it is hard to imagine how things could ever have been otherwise: we struggle today to conceive of sex in ways other than through the normative lens of consent. But it is objectively clear that this was not a prevalent way of thinking even within living memory, let alone in time periods or cultures that we know of in which coercing people into sex was not considered bad at all in and of itself (for example, child marriage or the sexual use of slaves are practices that are or have been considered entirely acceptable) and, conversely, when entirely consensual homosexuality was, or still is, punished by death.

One might think then that the paradigmatic sexual abnormality today would be rape qua the archetype of nonconsensual sex. However, I think it is quite clear that the most negatively regarded sexual behaviour today is not rape per se, but, more specifically, paedophilia, which is to say sexual assault on children by adults. This, I would suggest, is because paedophilia is not merely contingently nonconsensual, but a situation where consent is considered absolutely impossible. Children are deemed incapable of consenting to sex; hence, all sex with children is a priori rape. This puts paedophilia in a position in our normative order that is functionally isomorphic to the position of homosexuality in the previous normative order: the homosexual was the sexually abject subject insofar as their desire could never be the basis of reproductive marriage; the paedophile is sexually abject insofar as their desire could never be the basis of consensual sex. Zoophilia and necrophilia are of course also categories of sexual inclination involving entities incapable of consent, but these surely are not considered to be as heinous as paedophilia because animals and corpses have a lesser moral status than children.

That this abnormalization of nonconsent is the corollary of the normalization of homosexuality contradicts ongoing right-wing warnings (and very marginal positive arguments to this effect from the left) that LGBT+ rights are a slippery slope to the progressive normalization of paedophilia, zoophilia, etc. Right-wingers predict this, I would suggest, because they are working from an older normative paradigm in which consent is not the decisive factor in deciding what is or is not appropriate. Paedophilia in particular was, until recently, closely connected with homosexuality in the popular imagination (literally, 'paedophilia' etymologically means not 'sex with children' but the 'love of boys'), which is why, in an earlier phase of the gay liberation struggle, some gay activists prominently argued that paedophilia had to be normalized in order to normalize homosexuality. What has happened instead is that this link between homosexuality and paedophilia has largely been severed in the popular imagination. We can also point to increasing prohibition of zoophilia – to the progressive criminalization of sex between humans and animals across the United States during this century, for example – correlative with the decriminalization of sodomy.

Celibacy

Another dimension of the new normal in relation to sexuality – albeit a weaker and therefore less obviously desirable one than the focus on consent – is that actually having (consensual) sex is itself part of the norm. This is a subtle change inasmuch as the older norm also implied that people should have sex, but only relatively incidentally as part of a norm of reproductive marriage. Not getting married has now, by contrast, come to be considered almost normal – albeit partly because being in a relationship with a long-term partner outside marriage is considered almost equivalent to *de jure* marriage. Marriage, I think, remains ultimately normative – particularly since the extension of marriage to same-sex couples – because it is still the implicit telos of monogamous relationships, which in turn remain normative (as I will discuss below). But since marriage is now conceived as merely a final stage in a sexual relationship that begins well before marriage, it is considered normal to cohabit in a de facto marriage and even have children before marrying *de jure*. Since it is also normal now to divorce and repartner, going through the process again, it is no longer ever definitively abnormal to be unmarried. Something similar can be said about both non-cohabiting relationships and sexually active singleness: these have been normalized qua life stages, and though they may be regarded as abnormal beyond a certain age, they are not understood to be inherently problematic. By contrast, long-term adulthood *celibacy* (as opposed to mere singleness) has come to be regarded as effectively pathological. In the era of conformism, it was possible to deem sex outside marriage to be abnormal because norms were categorial. Sex was normal for the married and not for the unmarried. Such a division has since become untenable, and hence sex becomes normal for everyone, and celibacy by contrast abnormal for anyone.

One must distinguish celibacy here not only from singleness (which implies a lack of a permanent sexual relationship, not sexual abstinence) but also from asexuality. Celibacy implies having sexual desire but choosing not to act on it; asexuality implies lacking sexual desires altogether. Not having sexual desires at all is clearly very uncommon, but if one identifies as asexual, not having sex now clearly rates as normal behaviour by the reigning norm of expressing one's innate desires. Celibacy, by contrast, now amounts to an abnormal failure to express a determinate sexuality. A particular – albeit in many ways peculiar – indication of this effect can be found in the discourses both by and about so-called 'incels', a portmanteau of 'involuntary celibates'.

The term 'incel' has been adopted principally by young heterosexual men who cohered on the internet to describe their own sexual inactivity as something foisted on them by various social trends, most prominently feminism.[1] This fostered a considerable backlash, in which incels were pilloried, held responsible for their own lack of sexual success and mocked. While substantively correct, this reaction fundamentally concurred that these men's celibacy was abnormal, seeing it now though as indicative of their contemptibleness.

'Involuntary celibacy' is of course strictly speaking oxymoronic, since celibacy is, by definition, voluntary. The very fact that celibacy can be viewed as something involuntarily foisted on people, rather than figuring – as it historically had been in the Christian West – as a virtuous choice, indicates a change in the normative calculus, from seeing refraining from acting on sexual impulses as actively good, to seeing not acting on these impulses as a kind of failure. From this contemporary point of view, if anyone claims to be voluntarily celibate, this appears to be a kind of 'cope', by which the sexually unsuccessful claim to be choosing something that no one could want. While the critique of the incels amounts to the quite plausible claim that they are really *voluntarily* choosing to be celibate while falsely claiming that others are making this choice for them, their claim is in effect that all celibacy is involuntary since no one would really choose it. Here, among the incel community and related online masculinists, there is a strong influence of evolutionary biology that says that the innate purpose of people is to breed, which of course pushes their discourse in a strongly heteronormative, even homophobic, direction. The basic principle that people should have sex, that it is normal to have sex and therefore abnormal not to have sex beyond the age of consent is shared in common with the contemporary *Leitkultur*, however.

While the 'incel' is a *sui generis* category, I think we encounter, both in the concept itself and in the discourse about it, a general pathologization of celibacy. This pathologization is more or less unconscious, without any palpable deliberate intent – quite unlike the abnormalization of nonconsent. It follows ineluctably from the norm that one should express one's sexual desires. While, of course, at a legal level, gay liberation only means that engaging in same-sex sexual activity becomes normal to the extent that it is desired (that is, that it is consensual), the logic of this demand is that denying people the right to have sex is bad and, thus, that expressing one's (consensual) sexual inclinations in sexual acts is a positive good. Once sexual expression becomes normalized, not acting on one's sexual inclinations at all becomes abnormalized.

The abnormalization or denormalization of celibacy has a long history in the West. It unmistakably began in the sixteenth century with the Reformation, which ended clerical and monastic celibacy as social institutions in Northern Europe. Previously, chastity was unambiguously considered the more blessed state.[2] The Catholic Church has indeed continued to this day to uphold the Christian valorization of chastity initiated by the Apostles.[3] Thus, the contemporary Catholic Catechism, while it allows that some people are innately homosexual, owns that gay people are *eo ipso* 'called to chastity',[4] considering this an entirely virtuous option, indeed the only one for all people not specifically called to marry. The reigning contemporary norm, I am suggesting, is the inverse of this, namely that people are effectively called to express their sexuality, whatever it may be, in sexual acts; only asexuals can therefore be said to be called to chastity.

For this reason, sexual liberation has actually always had an uneasy relationship with the notion of consent. Sexual liberation only implies consent when it is governed by the liberal principle that differentiates liberty from licence, which is to say, says that we should only seek sexual liberation to the extent that it is compatible with the sexual liberation of others. Consent is thus the compromise that allows maximal societal sexual liberation. An alternative possible direction for the liberation of sex is offered in the thought of the Marquis de Sade, namely that everyone should have the right to have sex with anyone they want regardless of that person's objections – which would nonetheless, on Sade's view, be egalitarian inasmuch as anyone would freely be allowed to rape anyone else.[5] Incels themselves indeed tend in this Sadistic direction, effectively taking the promise of sexual fulfilment seriously, and consider the use of the norm of consent by women to deny them sex to be a betrayal of that promise. The concept of the incel developed around the paradoxical idea that if consensual sex is the norm, then lack of sex also ought to be consented to, and incels do not consent. This of course is not logically implied by the norm of consensual sex, and hints at the rejection of that norm in favour of a new idea of sex as a human right, one that explicitly nods to older ideas of the rights of men over their wives, but in fact is novel inasmuch as there was never previously any presumption that men were as such entitled to marry, only that men who were married were entitled to have sex with their wives. The incel's Sadism is thus a distinctively contemporary perspective.

This logic of sex as a right is seen also in the prominent claim in the ostensibly quite opposed discourse for the 'normalization' of 'sex work' in recent years that sex workers are necessary to allow for the expression of the sexuality of, for example, disabled people, who otherwise might not be able to have sex at all. This discourse around sex work still maintains the norm of consent, inasmuch as sex workers do consent on the basis of a financial transaction. This sits uneasily, however, with the idea of a right to sex: if it truly is a human right to have sex, it would seem unjust to deny it to anyone based on their inability to pay. The workaround here is for the state to pay via benefits to the disabled, for example[6] – a position effectively parodied (or even invoked unironically: it is hard to tell) by an incel meme demanding 'state-issued girlfriends'.

I believe there is a serious social issue to address here, but that it is not the one that incels diagnose themselves. That is, I do not think the problem is that young men need but cannot find an outlet for their sexual urges. This surely is a kind of problem, but also a relatively perennial one. Rather, I think the real issue is the sheer existence of the norm of sexual expression (along with existence of the internet), which has caused sexually frustrated young men to believe that it is not because of their youth that they are experiencing sexual frustration but rather because they are victims of a monstrous aberration that must be solved politically. The norm has generated the severe alienation clearly felt by incels, to psychotic and violent extremes in some prominent cases. My critique of the incel essentially is that he has wrongly identified his enemy as the normative demand for consent, rather than resisting the normative demand for sex that is amplifying his sexual frustration to an unbearable intensity.

Most people, however, simply take both dimensions of the norm to be unproblematically operative – that is, that there is an absolute requirement for consent to be obtained for sex to occur, and that people should act on their sexual desires by having sex. The two norms together produce a normative expectation that people be able to obtain consent for the sex they want to have. This allows them to malign incels for their abnormal failure to obtain consensual sex, evincing the very same normative frame that drives the incels' own rage. But it also recursively makes everyone alienated or worse – if not to the same extent as incels – when they inevitably do find their own desires frustrated.

Monogamy

If expression of sexual desire has become normal, how does monogamy remain normal, considering that it is inevitably premised on a suppression of excess sexual desire? Monogamy has historically been premised explicitly on the idea that the restriction of desire is virtuous, conceived within much of the Christian tradition as a (sometimes lesser) alternative to chastity. Yet, while Christianity has clearly declined precipitously in the West in recent decades, adultery has, in recent years, come to be popularly viewed as less and less acceptable.[7]

I would suggest this increased intolerance of 'cheating' correlates to a decreasing normative expectation that anyone establish a monogamous relationship in the first place: if you want to have sex with more than one person, this is now understood to be an acceptable lifestyle choice. Thus, if you do decide to get married, you are entirely blameworthy for transgressing this voluntary embrace of monogamy. Formerly, when heterosexual, monogamous marriage figured as the only legitimate vehicle for the expression of sexuality, straying and expressing one's sexuality sinfully outside wedlock was understood to be a likely, if nonetheless morally outrageous, occurrence. Now, marriage is seen merely as a lifestyle choice that suits those who are naturally inclined towards monogamy, hence one that no one should in principle choose if they have any wayward desires that might incline them to step outside its bonds. I have been told (by someone who considered themselves to be innately inclined to monogamy) that anyone who doesn't simply and naturally find themselves sexually attracted just to one person is inherently polyamorous and should not pursue a monogamous lifestyle. How many of us can truly say we attain such a norm?

Perhaps for precisely the reason that so few of us could meet it, such a stringent view of monogamy is still unusual at this point. Monogamy is perhaps the most resilient of the traditional norms qua norm. Rates of marriage are declining and divorce are rising, but people by and large divorce to pursue new monogamous relationships, and the unmarried still seem largely to pursue 'monogamy' through informal personal arrangements, so the basic form seems to remain alive, if not well. However, polyamory is increasingly, insistently posited as an acceptable alternative. The conscious practice of polyamory represents an attempt to square the circle of the apparent conflict between the diffusion of human sexual desires and the desire for secure relationships, by allowing people to form multiple loving attachments, with these attachments being consented to by all parties. The very idea of a compromise between desires is increasingly foreign to contemporary norms, such that people believe a priori that there must always be some arrangement that simultaneously allows full expression of all their desires. The idea that there might be some personal gain to be had through self-control and reticence is, by contrast, almost extinct. The norm of monogamy was traditionally not only about the inherent logic of a relationship, but was also a social norm, demanded for the sake of propriety and social stability. The new norms, by contrast, have no social dimension at all beyond the minimal liberal principle that one's actions should not directly harm others. For most people, however, polyamory still seems to lack intuitive appeal: it does not offer the surety of exclusive lifelong monogamy, and feelings of jealousy are a powerful countervailing force.

If there is increasing moral disapproval of adultery, there has been a dramatic collapse in formal controls on it: divorce has been made ever easier throughout the West and adultery has been decriminalized in all of Europe and more recently in most US states. If synchronic polyamory is still extremely unusual, what we might call diachronic polyamory is now the norm: having a single lifetime sexual partner is now considered abnormal, where previously it was considered the norm (especially for women), even if most people did not meet that norm in practice (but then most people never meet any operative norm in practice). The reason that having only one lifetime sexual partner is considered abnormal, on my account, is that it represents a failure to realize one's sexual desires, inasmuch as very few people can be said only to have been sexually attracted to one person during their lifetime.

Sex

Along with this has gone a general diminution of the significance of the family. The reigning norm of the family continues to be a biological one: everyone has a biological family, after all. There is certainly an insistence now that nonbiological families also be acknowledged and normalized, but this is not really particularly new. While the idea of a family comprising a same-sex couple and their children, where in most cases any given child is related biologically only to one of their two parents, has been normalized, this really differs in essence little, if at all, from a very long-lived model where a step-parent is regarded as the true parent of a biologically unrelated child of their spouse, or indeed from adoption of nonbiological children by straight couples. Once gay partnerships became normalized, normalization of their familial relations automatically followed. Such relations effectively ape the biological family model: they look like a heterosexual couple with their own biological children, and in fact thus fail to seriously call into question the biological familial norm. There are, as one might expect in our society, demands that individuals be allowed to decide what their familial relationships should be, to consent to them, as it were. The generic problem with this idea (championed in one interview by none other than Michel Foucault himself) is that, without the reference to biological relations, in our contemporary situation at least, there is nothing to differentiate it from mere friendship. The attempt to demand that the family be decisively freed from biological determinations thus ultimately, intentionally or not, pushes in the direction of the diminution of the form of the family. Thus, what has happened to the family has not been any serious change in its norm, but a massive devaluation of that norm: having a strong connection to one's family was once clearly normative. At this point, it is normal, in effect, not to have a family at all, even if, in a biological sense, this is strictly speaking impossible and hence not something one encounters in actuality.

Consent

Where the norm of following our own desires pulls us in the direction of polyamory, the norm of honouring the desires of others leads to demands for consent to be ever more explicit, and increasingly to recognize the possibility that it might be withdrawn at any time. I have no wish to question the principle of consent – as a modern liberal myself, I believe in it approximately as strongly as most people today. I rather mean to critique its elevation into a *norm*. The problem with consent as norm is the problem of all norms, namely that they push insistently towards an unreachably perfect apogee condemning all reality by contrasting it with an unobtainable image of perfection. Since absolute clarity can never be obtained, consent can never be absolute enough to evade suspicion. Even repeated explicit statements of consent from all parties would inevitably still allow for pauses between these declarations in which nonconsent might occur, and there will always be the suspicion that some or other declaration contains some ambiguity or is made without perfect consensuality, say through some asymmetry in power relations between parties – which in turn must always be present to a certain extent. The reality of the human mind is, moreover, such that we rarely if ever have a completely univocal preference in one direction, such that any consent is always accompanied by some feelings of reticence or misgiving. Thus, consent can never be total or perfect.

This problem of the unattainability of a norm of consent can be seen concretely in the 2018 furore around the published complaints of an anonymous woman about her sexual encounter with US comedian Aziz Ansari. She described the sex as consensual, but also as an assault. A crucial point in her account was that she did not know what she wanted from the encounter.[8] This is a perfectly plausible claim. However, there is no reason to believe that Ansari, for his part, had any more clarity than she did about what he wanted, or that such doubts can ever be entirely excluded.

In light of the intractability of such problems, Catharine MacKinnon's jurisprudential principle that sex should be understood as a prima facie injury is an obvious response. Much of what typically happens in sexual intercourse would in any other context today clearly be considered assault to the point that parties would not be deemed legally able to consent to it.[9] The norm of consent pushes towards a point where no sex can be considered normal, in a surprising but widely noted confluence with historic Christian teaching – although, more accurately, since orthodox Christianity explicitly has a loophole by which sex within marriage is not considered sinful, the final confluence would be with Gnosticism.[10] We can point here to the noticeable decline in the amount of sex people are actually having as indicating perhaps some societal turning away from sex.[11]

The tendency against sex, driven by a concern to completely prevent anyone ever being made to do anything they do not want, is, however, powerfully contradicted and checked by the opposite dimension of the norm that people should do whatever they want. One obvious way to square the contradiction here is through the production of realistic artificial (for example robotic) objects to allow full expression of sexual desires. The problem with that move is, as the French philosopher Maurice Merleau-Ponty pointed out, that we only desire to objectify people sexually because they are subjects, that is, for most people at least, sexual desire includes a desire to have sex with real people, not with merely human-like objects.[12]

Queer

I am suggesting then that, today, we are caught on the horns of a norm that demands the total satisfaction of all sexual desires, which is unachievable for the trivial reason (one that affects all such norms) that complete satisfaction is not possible for anyone, and the specific reason that satisfaction will never be entirely mutual (even to the extent it exists at all) where multiple parties are concerned, whereas sexual desire inherently points towards the involvement of multiple persons.

Foucault's solution to the vicissitudes of sexuality (albeit that he identifies rather different ones from those I describe here) in the first volume of his *History of Sexuality* was not to push for some new norm of sex, nor even for the abolition of norms around sex in general, but rather, in effect, for the abolition (or at least the minimization) of the concept of sex itself as such. This applies not only to questions of sexuality, but also to those around what is today called 'gender'.[13] I commend readers to read Foucault for themselves, but, to state his thesis in an extremely simplified form, he argues that our society has put too much emphasis on sex in myriad ways, and hence that getting rid of the idea of sex would allow us to refocus on what is really important.

There has been a serious effort in the direction of defying norms in relation to sex and sexuality under the name of 'queerness'. Particularly in its more intellectual form, so-called 'queer theory', this has been seminally influenced by Foucault's thought. Such a defiance of the norm is, however, easier to declare than to practise. While once to be gay or trans was to be abnormal, hence queer, today these identities have been intensely normalized, such that it is possible to assert that one is a normal gay man or lesbian, who is not queer, a married gay man or lesbian, a family gay man or lesbian. Queerness then becomes a kind of rump identity for those who refuse sexual norms as such. In the end, I am sceptical that there is much space left for this strategy to operate. Queers are no longer *doing* anything that is deemed norm-violating. There is certainly no palpable enthusiasm among queer-identifying people to engage in practices still considered abnormal, which is to say nonconsensual sex or chastity, nor should there be. Queerness thus begins to amount only to the refusal of sexual categorization as such. However, this gesture itself has been co-opted by being considered a sexual category in its own right, embodied in the addition of a Q to LGBT to make LGBTQ. Queerness is simply rendered one sexual identity among others despite its very essence being the refusal of such categorization. In gender politics, much as with sexuality, the leading tendency seems to be the indefinite profusion of nonetheless discrete gender identities, among which the refusal of gender constituted by identifying as genderqueer comes to operate as an additional gender pigeonhole. Thus queerness, the generic refusal of normality, has come to be normalized.

Sex

Gender

I have suggested that the overarching norm in relation to sexuality today is effectively gender-neutral; while gender-attractedness remains the defining dimension of sexuality, different attractions are now considered equal before the norm. This change follows a general trend for norms to cease being gender-specific. This is not to say that there are no longer any gender-based norms. As we saw in the case of sexuality, there are actually more norms than ever. The pattern, however, is for supervening norms to become gender-neutral, while gender-based norms become increasingly ephemeral, even if they become more profuse. Today, for example, it is normal for women, but not for men, to shave their legs and wear makeup, but such norms are literally superficial, even if there is nonetheless a feminist case for criticizing them as discriminatory (and indeed also cases for criticizing them as homo- and transphobic). Norms that remain gender-based seem either to have to do with biological facts that are as yet largely ineluctable – so it remains normal for women to be shorter than men, less hairy than men, able to have children, and menstruate (even if these norms are increasingly in doubt in ways that I will deal with below) – or ones that have little substantive importance – so it is normal for women, but not men, to have long hair and wear a skirt. All these norms are longstanding, in place for a century at least. Over that century, however, women have ceased to be excluded from norms of substantive import: it is now normal for them to vote and drink with their friends in public and have jobs when married, which indicates that previously male-only norms have been extended to apply to women in relation to recreation, employment and civic engagement. Female-only norms have not, conversely, been applied to men, however; indeed, there has been little effort to make that happen, because they were not deemed desirable or significant. So, although there have been some trends for more men to wear their hair long and get their ears pierced, these remain marginal phenomena. In relation to more substantive questions, there have been changes. In particular, it has become normal for men to engage in housework and childcare to a greater extent. Though it remains normal for women to do more of these tasks than men, it is abnormal for a man now to do absolutely no housework or childcare, although this previously had been precisely the male norm. The continuing extent to which it remains normal for women to do the bulk of domestic labour of course constitutes an ongoing point of contention for feminists who push for the demolition of continuing gender inequity in this sphere.

The situation I outline here has been increasingly complicated by the ongoing normalization of being transgender, which to a greater extent than ever before is opening up the norms of femininity and masculinity themselves to everyone in principle. By this I do not mean the facile suggestion that now anyone can simply declare themselves to be male or female – though this is in a sense ultimately the case, as I will go on to discuss. Rather, the discourse around the phenomenon of being transgender has opened up male and female norms to all not so much by allowing persons to transition between one gender and another, but by allowing that any individual may determine how they will express the gender with which they identify. That is, while gender increasingly becomes a matter of self-identification, this identification is itself denormativized – by which I mean that there is less and less any norm governing any posited identity. One may in principle identify as male, but nonetheless be feminine, potentially even in every applicable way. The alternative is to hold trans people up to gender norms that they will likely, on average, fail to approximate as closely as cis people do. The impetus to fully accept trans people as being of their identified gender, no different from cis people of that gender, regardless of the trans person's gender expression, pushes in the direction of the final elision of male and female gender norms.[14]

Of course, this logic is still quite far from the actual normative situation that obtains today. In actuality, norms that people of a given biological sex should have a corresponding gender presentation and behaviour are still largely operative, often to a crushing extent. For all that it is forcefully asserted that it should be considered normal for someone to be transgender, I think we are kidding ourselves if we believe our society is at anything like the point where transgender men giving birth, for example, is actually generally regarded as normal, though surely it is vastly more accepted than hitherto, to the extent also that people are generally quite likely to mask any feeling they may have that this is abnormal.

There has been a major shift in attitudes towards the phenomenon of being transgender, though not yet one so complete as the shift in attitudes towards sexuality. It is much harder to track changes in attitudes towards being transgender than towards homosexuality, because surveys relating to the former are a relatively recent phenomenon. The evidence suggests, however, that transgender people today are broadly accepted as such in the West. A 2018 global survey by Ipsos found a majority of people across the surveyed countries agreeing with the statement that transgender people 'are a natural occurrence'. This varied from clear majorities in some countries (such as Spain, where 64 per cent of surveyed people agreed with this assessment) to thin minorities (the lowest proportion of people to agree with this proposition in a Western country was in Italy, where only 45 per cent agreed – so still close to half of respondents). Clear majorities of those surveyed in every Western country agreed that they 'wanted our country to do more to support and protect transgender people'.[15]

The wording in terms of transgender people 'being a natural occurrence' is, in my view, highly indicative and revealing. I imagine many might object to characterizing any people as an 'occurrence' – and this might in part explain why this phrase garnered less support than the broader expression of support for transgender people. The fact that the phrasing in different languages would carry different connotations might also explain some of the variability in the responses. Nevertheless, I tend to think that believing something to be *natural* and believing it to be *normal* are more or less the same thing today – even if I also think there may be serious divergence between what people say they believe and what they actually (perhaps unconsciously) believe. Today, if we believe that x is natural, we by that token take x to be a norm. This does not, however, make us normative naturalists, conforming our norms with what science tells us; rather, it means the inverse, that we believe that there must be an objective, empirical, scientific basis to whatever norms we posit. Indeed, arguments that invoke nature are inevitably to some extent guilty of the naturalistic fallacy: what is can never be a basis for arguing about what should be the case, inasmuch as everything that is is *eo ipso* natural. Hence, the debate (if this is not too civil a term to describe such bitter and polemical exchanges) around the normality of homosexuality has tended to involve each side effectively proclaiming that homosexuality either is or is not natural. We see the pattern replicated today in relation to a 'debate' around gender. From the right, biological facts about sex are pointed to in order to assert that conventional gender divisions and native biological sexual characteristics should be maintained. From the left, it is now hegemonically asserted that scientific biology supports understandings of gender as on a spectrum and as mutable.

Identity

The concept 'transgender' involves the possibility of a misalignment between a person's gender identity and biological sex. Having initially been conceived as a psychiatric condition that must be medically diagnosed, the impossibility of objectively determining whether or not someone has gender dysphoria, along with growing resistance to the idea that being transgender be considered a mental illness, has led to the acceptance of the principle that a person's own reports of their gender are inerrant. This shift is part and parcel of the normalization of being transgender: the previous framing of 'transgenderism' as a mental disorder clearly meant understanding it as an axiomatically abnormal condition; if being transgender is normal, it cannot be a matter for differential diagnosis, but rather must be understood as a natural fact, as biological sex has historically been understood to be. It is also part and parcel of the new general norm that individuals are uniquely and infallibly capable of discerning their authentic essence. This has fed into the conceptual division of sex and gender, with each now understood to be in its own way manifest and natural, but distinct from one another. Each moreover has its own norms: retention of a notion of biological sex allows a maintenance of the medical norms pertaining to each sex, while taking sexually differentiated social norms to be something that apply based on 'gender' alone regardless of biological sex.

The explicit reason people are allowed to determine their own gender identity is not that they have any right to *choose* that identity – since this is absolutely not considered a matter of volition at all – but rather that they are the only ones competent to discern what their *natural* gender actually is. In practice, however, this does mean that it is possible to choose one's gender, simply because there is no way of knowing whether there is a volitional component in anyone's self-identification. I do not claim that many or even any people who claim to be transgender definitely are actually engaging in deception or even wishful thinking in this way. Rather, my point is simply that no one can know whether or not this may sometimes be the case, or indeed how frequently. This is an endemic epistemic problem with the contemporary principle that people should be believed absolutely in relation to their reports of their own experience wherever this principle applies.

This reliance on subjects' self-reports of their identity might seem to be a victory of Canguilhem's suggested route for the determination of the norm. Note, though, that Canguilhem assigned only a limited normative role to the subject: on his account, a patient can inerrantly tell us that they are sick – that is, not normal – but this does not mean they should be trusted to diagnose unerringly what their sickness is. If someone says they are having difficulties in relation to their gender identity, it is surely likely that they are. It does not follow, however, that their belief that they have an inherent gender at variance with their biology is infallible. Such a conclusion would run counter to the basic diagnostic insight of psychoanalysis that the presentation of a psychological problem conceals its deep cause. This is not to say that patients' claims about themselves are necessarily false, only that no one has inerrant, or even particularly accurate, understandings of themselves. While we do have some privileged information about ourselves that no one else can have, we also lack the critical distance in relation to ourselves that others have. My conclusions about myself are thus certainly not always right, and indeed there is important information about myself to which I am peculiarly blind. Yet, our contemporary norms involve understanding ourselves to be self-sufficient individuals responsible for our own satisfaction. The basic fact that individuals and their desires are constituted in complicated, social ways that elude anyone's full understanding runs contrary to this.

This is not to suggest that any older norm is better. The foregoing normative situation involved the opposite error of overriding subjective experience based on supposedly objective medical norms, applied by supposedly inerrant medicos. The medical normalization of gender has a horrific history. Nor am I urging some radical rejection of the concept of being transgender so much as a more cautious approach towards gender identification than is currently being allowed by advocates of transgender rights, which in practical terms implies a greater emphasis on psychological counselling as an invariable accompaniment to any physiological intervention. Of course, this might sound like a peculiar pathologization of trans people, following the old logic of categorization of gender dysphoria as a mental illness. But my point is nothing so much as asserting the precautionary principle: if one is going to undergo a surgical intervention, this should be approached with caution rather than with blind trust in the infallibility and durability of people's cognitive states. This is not to say that there is a generic issue with transitioning, but rather that there may always be things that are not known in such a decision, and that one thus should proceed cautiously, simply because one's actual reaction to a changed situation, no matter how certain one feels about a decision, is radically unpredictable. The generic problem that the precautionary principle responds to is the unreliability of any inference on the basis of experience.

Similarly, the primary issue I mean to highlight here is not specifically about the phenomenon of being transgender, but the more general development of a society that has radically rejected the historical pattern of an individual's identity being principally determined by extrinsic, sociocultural principles, in favour of ascribing to the individual an absolute right and inerrant ability to determine who they are. Something that might be said to be more basic than the right to determine one's gender in this regard is the right to determine one's own name. The freedom to call oneself whatever one wants is hardly entirely new – just as, historically, there has generally been no formal legal impediment against declaring oneself to be of whatever gender one liked. This is simply because, until relatively recently, there was no centralized registration of either names or genders in the first place. Any ability to define oneself then depended not on bureaucratic rules but on community recognition. While one was thus in principle free to self-nominate, self-nomination carried no decisive weight. Ultimately, the name one was called was always a social decision, made by those who spoke to and about a person, of whom that person themselves was an instance. Communities typically had both formal procedures for conferring names – the procedure in Western societies is the nomination of a person by their parents, until recently usually with the guidance and agreement of a priest – as well as less formal processes of nicknaming that sees names or cognomens accrue to individuals. While it has always been possible for an individual to declare that they have a new name, for this to have any effect it was necessary for people around them to use it to refer to them. This meant that renaming oneself historically was easiest in situations where an individual left one community and arrived in a different one where they had no previously recognized name. The bureaucratization of nomination clearly adds an impediment to changing one's name, if a rather trivial one in most jurisdictions. However, it also adds an official force to the change. While individuals in interpersonal contexts are not necessarily strictly bound to use someone's name simply because it is official, the onus has been radically moved from the community to determine an individual's name to the individual being able to self-nominate via the movement of authority from the community to the state. Something analogous has more lately happened in relation to gender.

To us today, this right to determine what other people call us might seem like freedom from the whimsy of our parents who gave us our original legal names or the pettiness of schoolyard bullies who gave us unflattering nicknames. While we may have good reason to reject the determination of our identity by such procedures, believing that individuals' identity can be determined by those individuals themselves simply implies a false ontology of the individual and a false account of how beliefs emerge. It means imagining that our self-nominations emerge from within us, rather than being socially determined, as they inevitably must be, even when we do not think they are. That is, the idea that we can name ourselves by an act that genuinely makes us sovereign over our identity is an illusion. It is illusory in much the same way that Napoleon's self-coronation was. That event indeed presages the emergence of the norm of self-sovereignty and our associated late modern form of subjectivity. We are all little Napoleons now, in effect.

Our own logic for our self-determination of course is not explicitly Napoleonic, but rather one of rational self-discovery. In naming ourselves, we are animated perhaps by a search for our true name – that we don't typically say as much is due perhaps to the fact that names are clearly arbitrary designators. But neither are many willing to say that they have simply arbitrarily invented a name for themselves to assure themselves of their autonomy. A clue to the nature of the shift in the understanding of nomination is offered, I think, by the recent shift in the historic practice by which names belonged to particular languages. That is, in the past, personal first names varied in spelling and pronunciation between European languages, such that someone called John in England would be called Jean in France and vice versa. Now, it is typically held that one's name is invariant and must be spelled and pronounced the same way even as one moves into linguistic contexts with different phonetics and orthographies, just as individuals within a given language community seem increasingly to be named with no regard for the conventions of that language. Similarly, places used to have different names in different languages, such that a major city would have exonyms in the lexicons of neighbouring countries. So, Milano in Italy was called 'Milan' by the French and

'Mailand' by German speakers. Increasingly, however, such practices are frowned upon, and countries and cities assert the right to be called globally by their own local toponyms. The name, identity and individuality of the subject and object are all elevated above context.

Indeed, it seems to me that there is a much deeper epistemological stance in play here above this absolutization of the nomination of individual things. Much more than merely everyone knowing themselves perfectly, absolute transparency in both understanding the world and communicating that knowledge has come to be considered normal, which means both that it is considered ultimately desirable and that it is thought to be the commonplace default. Foucault notes that in modernity people cease to imagine they need to go through a process of development to gain wisdom, but rather imagine that the world is equally understandable by every human subject.[16] While the Habermasian 'ideal speech situation'[17] might indeed seem like a worthy goal, it is one we cannot actually expect to meet and certainly do not do so in practice. However, the nature of norms is such that people now imagine that perfect communication is operative in practice. The prevalence of the notion of 'gaslighting' today in part indicates the existence of an epistemic norm of transparency such that when there are, inevitably, either disagreements between people about their understanding of reality or serious deficiencies in interhuman communication, one party will claim that the other has deliberately misled them.

5

Life

This chapter deals with the most central issue there is in relation to norms. At its most general, given in the title of this chapter, this issue is one of life itself. Life in our society both operates as a norm and is itself subject to norms. There has never been a society before that has placed as much value on biological life, on keeping its people alive. This is part and parcel of what Foucault called our 'biopolitics'.[1] The extent to which life is the *sine qua non* of contemporary politics has been demonstrated in the extraordinary response to the coronavirus pandemic that broke out in 2020, with unprecedented restrictions on civic freedoms and constriction of economies in the name of defending life from harm.

As discussed in Chapter 1, the very form of the norm might have originated in efforts to protect life from disease. Medicine is certainly the main vector by which the model of the norm has spread throughout our societies since the eighteenth century. The rootedness of our conception of the normal in health perhaps has deep implications. The model of the norm is certainly not far from that of the cure. For every ill that assails us personally and socially, we tend to believe there must be a solution, a perfection that will remove all unpleasantness. When put starkly like this, I suspect many would agree that such panaceas are impossible, but ordinarily we are not made to face up to this impossibility, and rather simply act as if all our problems can and should be solved. Indeed, I expect some actually will argue that, yes, all the problems of the world can be cured and to say otherwise is at best rank defeatism and at worst actively taking the side of those problems. For centuries now, scientific and technological progress has seemed to hold out this hope, but I will maintain that it is, in a strict sense, impossible ever to attain normative perfection.

Health is a norm explicit in medicine and now taken up throughout society. Connectedly, life itself – in the sense of being organically alive – is a prevalent norm. This norm is of course implied by health inasmuch as we can hardly be healthy if we are dead, although, as I will discuss below, the norm of health can be taken to imply that unhealthy lives should be terminated, so there can be a tension between these two norms even from a strictly medical standpoint. Neither of these norms is peculiar to the new normal of authentic hedonist individualism. Rather, they are longstanding in modernity. However, our contemporary norms certainly imply health – inasmuch as following our desires generally requires being healthy – and a fortiori imply life inasmuch as we need to be alive to meet any of our more specific contemporary norms. However, the norm of health and hence that of life frequently run up against our norm of expressing ourselves by following our desires where what we desire is deleterious to our health. These intractable difficulties of reconciling the norm of pleasure with the norm of

Life

life will constitute the principal object of discussion in this chapter.

Anxiety

With the decline of religion in late modernity, spiritual concerns have receded, and physical health and wellbeing have become more dominant concerns. After all, if this is the only life we have, the only game would seem to be to try to prolong and improve it as best we can. These concerns provide us with two norms, one of perfect health, the other of perfect enjoyment. These are hardly unrelated: being unhealthy may be presumed to reduce one's enjoyment, and failing to enjoy life is, moreover, in itself ultimately understood to constitute a mental health problem, which in turn is likely to have a negative impact on our physical health. That said, there is also often a tension between these two norms, inasmuch as what we enjoy doing is often bad for our health. A prime example of this is the extent to which foods we enjoy eating tend to be precisely the ones that harm us. Indeed, diet is a privileged point of intersection of these two concerns in the West today and hence a pervasive source of anxiety for us. The notion of 'guilt' today is frequently explicitly attached not to immoral behaviour but to unhealthy eating, indicating the extent to which concern about food has displaced religion and morality.

In this regard, we may seem to have come full circle, back to the Western culture that preceded Christianity: in classical Antiquity, people were similarly more preoccupied with diet than almost anything else.[2] The ancients, like us, were very concerned about the healthiness of their food. What they didn't have, I would suggest, is our norm-based conception of health. The ancients' limited understanding of nutrition meant they could feel relatively assured they were eating the right thing in the right situation, and had only a fraction of our conception of the possible negative consequences of not doing so. We would now say that much of what they believed about this was wrong, and that we have a much greater chance of understanding what it is healthy to eat, but perversely it seems entirely likely that our diet is actually less healthy than the Mediterranean diet of classical antiquity. Moreover, no one today can ever be sure that they are eating healthily to the extent that the ancients could. If someone today feels fully assured that their diet is entirely healthful, it can only be out of ignorance: once one actually starts digging into the scientific literature on nutrition (let alone the obliquely related advice that proliferates online and in popular publications), one readily encounters enough contradictory information to cast doubt on any specific diet.

At this point, in the West, most of us are justifiably more concerned about eating too much than too little. A paradox of this is that such anxieties contribute to a general level of stress in our lives that drives us to seek comfort in eating more and unhealthy food. This is compounded by the fact that being anxious is itself considered abnormal, despite the fact that it is a ubiquitous feature of human existence. This leads anxiety always to be reflexively doubled in our society: since all anxiety is abnormal, it is itself a source of additional anxiety about itself, hence all anxiety experienced in the age of norms (and I would suggest there is already more of it than was ever generally the case before) is automatically magnified relative to any equivalent anxiety in the past. Norms are not the source of all our anxiety, but they are a great multiplier of it.

Just as norms that induce anxiety abnormalize that very anxiety, so the same norms do not expect us to go through the process of self-excoriation in order to become healthy that they effectively demand of us. Rather, we are expected always already to be spontaneously healthy. We are all familiar with the images used to advertise healthy food: smiling, happy people, without a care in the world, slim and healthy-looking, eating with friends, al fresco in the summer sunlight. This deliberately belies the reality of healthy eating, which is born of anxiety, is often antisocial and causes conflicts with others who would prefer to eat less healthily, and which is typically experienced as a privation and self-denial that makes people miserable, perhaps even when they claim that it does not. A particular irony is that anxiety, asociality and misery are themselves genuinely unhealthy. And we are not unaware of this. Indeed, we are aware that, as we are trying to meet one norm, we are violating others and we shouldn't be living this way.

Anorexia is perhaps the ultimate product of out-of-control spiralling of anxiety about diet. Anorexics are so concerned with eating too much that they starve themselves, but this reaction makes them feel worse than ever: they are aware at some level that their anorexia is abnormal, even as, at a more decisive level, they continue to believe themselves to be overweight. Anorexia is either an entirely new disease or, at the very least, one that is vastly more common today than ever before, and I of course suspect that the paradoxical compulsion of the norm is implicated in this. Different cases of anorexia probably relate to different norms in different ways. By common consensus, so-called 'body image' is important here – which, in my terms, is a norm for the body. A simplistic way of reading anorexia in relation to the norm, which may be more or less accurate

Life

in some specific cases, is that it is an extreme devotion to a norm of skinniness by which one can never be skinny enough, which indeed tends towards absolute nonexistence. Until recently, the dominant norm of feminine beauty seemed to be one associated with catwalk models in which a woman exists almost solely as a clothes horse – without form or mass, tall and slender and utterly unobtrusive. In part because of concerns that such a norm was driving eating disorders, there has been a palpable and impactful reaction against the norm of skinniness. This has formally been to celebrate all women's body types, but in practice has dovetailed with a significant shift in the norm of feminine beauty from skinniness to voluptuousness. However, there is no clear evidence that this shift in body norm has reduced rates of eating disorders. This leads me to suspect that it does not matter which precise body image is normative. Qua norm, any such image is unreachable for anyone, and hence drives anxiety. I suspect eating disorders may thus be a more generalized reaction to the impossibility of finding an optimal diet, which is to say a kind of total rejection of the norm itself, reacting to this by turning against eating altogether.[3]

Diet

It is not considered normal to eat things that are deleterious to one's health, but, as I have indicated, there is never any verifiable point at which we can know we have reached maximal healthiness, because there is disagreement about exactly what constitutes healthy eating. This means that people who are actively trying to eat maximally healthily will always have to shift their diet in search of an unachievable finality.

However, even if we disregard marginal nitpicking disagreements about its actual healthiness, following the diet that scientific consensus deems maximally healthy today – rich in leafy greens and whole grains, containing no processed foods, and very little animal fat – could not be considered fully normal because of the existence of countervailing norms other than that of health. In fact, following an entirely healthy diet, never eating any of the myriad commonplace foods that are incompatible with such a diet, would seem weird, even risible, to most people. This might seem to be a case of this diet not being normal in the different sense of being average – and it certainly is extremely atypical – but it also contravenes various deep-seated cultural ideas concerning which food is appropriate. Such cultural ideas provide significant normative support from the countervailing norm of enjoyment. Food is supposed to be utterly healthful, but also utterly enjoyable – and what is considered pleasant fare is culturally constituted. In reality, we are acutely aware that there is a pay-off between healthiness and deliciousness, but this does not relieve us from the absolute imperative to meet both norms.

Norms of health and enjoyment are further complicated by the existence of norms pertaining to food itself. What we eat must not only be perfect in taste (which of course correlates to enjoyment) and healthiness, but also in appearance. Perhaps 20 per cent of the food produced in the United States, if not more, is discarded because it is cosmetically imperfect.[4] The contemporary aestheticization of food follows both the major normative axes in relation to diet, visible in the 'food porn' shared on social media. On the one hand, one sees vegan health food made to look maximally appealing to the eye – for example 'superfoods' juxtaposed with one another in colourful so-called 'Buddha bowls'. On the other hand, in the very same period that veganism has been gaining in popularity, there has been a trend towards artisanal 'dude food' – burgers, pizzas and desserts in particular. Instagram accounts showcase grotesquely outsize single menu items containing a day's worth of calories. We attempt to reach, on the one hand, perfection in the visual representation of healthy eating and, on the other, perfection through images that intimate desirable flavour and texture.

Veganism of course does not present itself as merely a health fad; today, it can be characterized as a significant ethical movement. Ethical veganism is nevertheless really a case in point of the new norms, clearly representing a rebellious stance, positioning its adherents against mainstream Western culinary practices. But in doing so, it follows reigning norms such as the liberal harm principle (that we should only follow our desires insofar as this does not harm others – now understood to incorporate harm towards animals as well as humans), naturalness (vegans are generally at pains to claim a vegan diet is natural, even though this is irrelevant to any of their other claims for its benefits) and healthiness (vegans will not admit that their diet might not be entirely healthy, presumably in part because its ethical basis is usually rooted in an idea of harm minimization that would preclude its practitioners from harming their own health by following it). Veganism is unlike other new normative stances discussed here, in that it is still generally thought of as abnormal: it remains normal to eat meat today, since the harm principle is generally not extended to all animals, and since it is clearly enjoyable to eat meat. While vegans often claim that they do not sacrifice enjoyment, non-vegans generally do not believe them, and hence veganism has been unable to become normative. However much advocates of healthy eating might claim that vegan wholefoods are delicious – and while they indeed can be – the claim that healthy fare is more tasty than a bacon cheeseburger rings hollow for most people.

While health food and junk food are to some extent the preserves of different lifestyle groups, for most people they coexist as forces pulling in different directions, and as a result we today tend to alternate between the virtue of health and the vice of junk. Indeed, in some fashionable contemporary eateries, the two extremes coexist on the same menu. It has been incarnated too in the contradictory lifestyle of the millennial hipster: a boozy all-night drug binge, a meal of deep-fried food, followed by a detox, kale and quinoa, and a trip to the gym. While such a lifestyle may in the end approach a balance (the kind one might also have by simply eating a conventional diet and engaging in moderate exercise), and indeed in its wild extremes may in the best-case scenario serve to satisfy the human subject, who craves both transgressive excess and anal-retentive self-correction, I would suggest it fails to avert anxiety. In the end, we will always justifiably feel we are missing out on deliciousness when we eat healthily and are harming ourselves when we eat deliciously.

Ultimately, we are always being pushed to square the circle in our attempts to be simultaneously healthy and sybaritic. In every society, there is a dialectic of feasting and restraint, but in our society of the norm this has become impossible. Restraint itself is no longer valorized as such; rather, only the feast is normal – except that the feast must somehow not involve overeating that might then require remediation. Hence our demonstrable mass tendency to eat in a way that is not only not maximally healthy, but does not even meet baseline levels of healthiness, which is to say that we simply eat too much on an ongoing basis. While some do find a kind of balance between excess and health, this is an atypically healthy outcome today: most people overeat more and more all the time, and food with poor nutritional content at that.

Part of this is surely due to changes in our material circumstances. Where our ancestors sometimes struggled to find enough to eat, and delicious fare could a fortiori only be enjoyed occasionally by dint of its unavailability, now deliciousness undreamt of before mechanized production is on sale at the checkout for a dollar per thousand kilojoules. In the past, codes governed when to fast and when to feast. These had developed in relation to rhythms of the seasons and cycles of life, sculpting necessities into meaningful rituals. As the availability of food increased, the cultural practices that grounded abstemiousness and held back feasting – the Christian logic of contrition and fasting, for example – themselves all but disappeared. Christmas and Easter, the two greatest Christian feasts, are the sole widely kept remainders of the liturgical calendar in our secular age. Christian practice originally only allowed such feasts as the end point of long seasons of fasting.[5] Now they are effectively days on which people eat even more decadently than the already excessive eating they do on ordinary days. For the healthy eater, they are days when they face additional pressure to violate the norm of nutrition. That it remains normal to celebrate at Christmas and Easter is perhaps a case of the increasingly marginal influence of religious tradition allowing the norm of pleasure to overpower that of healthiness on such occasions. However, I think what this tends to indicate is not so much the resilience of religion as the extent to which hedonism tends to trump health. Clearly, the facts bear this out given that most of us clearly live lifestyles that are to some extent unhealthy because we are following our desires and chasing pleasure. This might reflect nothing so much as the trivial fact that, in a battle between the abstract idea of healthiness and an immediate desire to eat chocolate, the latter is very likely to win out. But our contemporary average fatness also reflects the loss of a serious countervailing force to our native drive towards self-indulgence. The norm of health does not provide it, since, after all, life and health are only attractive to the extent that they allow us to do something we want to do, and increasingly all we want to do is indulge ourselves. At a certain point, people shrug and say, OK, maybe drinking or smoking or eating bacon or riding motorcycles will harm me, but in the end what is the point of life if we are not to enjoy it? Few people genuinely and wholeheartedly endorse such a position, but I think it plays a powerful role in people's behaviour as a frequent thought at moments of decision, when yielding to the desire to eat cake or order another pint of beer. Those who live relatively healthy lifestyles today typically do so because they have found ways to take pleasure in things that are broadly in line with those lifestyles, have managed to practise healthiness in ways that give them adequate enjoyment. As long as we feel OK, then, we might conscientiously preserve our health, but the moment we do not, we seek solace in unhealthy behaviours.

This, I think, is due to the loss of a sense of individuality that placed us above desire satisfaction, as well as a loss of any higher purpose that would enjoin *ascesis*. We can now compute deferral only if it is presented as somehow leading to a tangible benefit. Having been more or less abolished as a practice of spiritual asceticism in our societies, fasting has in recent years been rediscovered as a fashionable health practice. The old bases of fasting – the spiritual benefits and material necessities – disappeared, but then new studies began to indicate that fasting increases health and longevity. On this basis, fasting was instantly renormalized within the new normative framework, essentially becoming just another form of the general voluntary restriction of diet for health. There is no thought that the denial of pleasure or desire associated with fasting might be a good thing, only that self-denial can be an overall positive because it will ultimately make us healthier and therefore able to enjoy life more for longer. Restriction is allowable on condition it makes the feast, when it comes, more enjoyable and guilt-free.

As with the conflict between norms of individualism and hedonism, when it comes to the norms of life and health there is similarly a general unwillingness to acknowledge the existence of a payoff between health and either pleasure or individuality. The difference here though is that the norm of health is not quite coequal, but an older yet nonetheless junior partner that must always justify itself in terms of enhancing pleasure and individuality. Given the extent to which the norm of health is embedded in the biopolitical infrastructure of our societies, we might reasonably expect it to outlast the spume of our contemporary norms, but it nonetheless must at least appear to submit to them.

Epidemiology

Still, even if framed in terms of a long-term hedonic calculus, it is hard for our culture to tolerate even temporary deferrals of satisfaction. The elusive goal of our society is to find a path that somehow concedes nothing in terms of desire satisfaction. As noted above, advertising is both indicative, and itself a major cause, of all this: almost every food product is sold – however improbably – as a supplement to a perfectly healthy lifestyle. McDonald's advertisements show smiling, youthful, slim actors gleefully eating their fare. The message here is 'this is normal' – not in the sense that ordinary fat, middle-aged, ugly people do it, but in the sense that people who are perfect do it. Such messages are pushing on an open door in a culture that validates desire qua desire. When I crave fatty and salty food, I think not only that I want to eat it, but that I *should* eat it. If I don't, it is likely only because it conflicts with another norm, such as ideals of health, longevity and body form. Advertising serves precisely to occlude such conflicts by misleading us into believing that any given product is compatible with every relevant norm. Of course, this cannot entirely silence the voice of conscience that reminds us that the norms are not ever actually being met. After all, health advocacy itself has an advertising budget.

The radical solution to such conflict would be to dispense entirely with one or more norms. There is a contemporary tendency effectively to abrogate the norm of health entirely via an appeal to the norm of expressing our essential natures. I am thinking specifically of the push-back against norms applied to bodies in favour of 'body positivity'. In particular, health messages have been cast as 'fat-shaming', or sometimes, conversely, as 'skinny-shaming'. The inverse of 'fat-shaming' is 'fat-acceptance', which consists in the normalization of fatness. Being fat really cannot become fully normal, however, unless medical normality is redefined – which may yet happen – or simply entirely ignored and the fat-acceptance movement generally seems unwilling to dismiss the norm of health entirely. Rather, its discourse insists implausibly that being fat can be healthy, a contestation that seems doomed always to face considerable tension unless medicine can be made to assess health by measures other than longevity and activity. For the moment, we simply see a confrontation between an insistent epidemiological discourse demanding people change their lifestyles to head off an epidemic of obesity and a discourse that demands forlornly that people not be made to feel bad about their weight.

The bottom line here is that accepting that pleasurable activity can be inherently unhealthy (which is surely true and obvious) means allowing that pleasure is doubled by unpleasure. This complication is unacceptable to a norm of pleasure, and there are thus two solutions: we can deny that a given pleasure is unhealthy, or we can deny that it really counts as a form of pleasure. This is the ultimate position of the enlightened healthy hedonist, who denies that unhealthy food can be truly pleasurable. This is no less repressive or delusional a stance though than the person who denies that unhealthy food is really unhealthy.

Of course, there is ample scope for individuals to object that epidemiological norms do not apply in their own instances for various reasons. The determination of whether people are overweight and the likely impact of this on their health are dependent on generalizations – such as the Body Mass Index – that do not apply equally to everyone. However, that such norms often do not apply in particular cases does not and cannot imply that such norms should not apply as they are intended to, which is to say across a population.

At this point, though, a rather different if interrelated normative conflict heaves into view. Relating to the conflict of health and enjoyment, though not exactly coinciding with it, is a conflict between norms of public good and individual freedom. This conflict is intensely politicized on a left–right axis, with the right today largely championing the cause of individual freedom against what they see as a left-wing 'nanny state'. A clear concrete example of this has been an attempt by New York City to limit portion sizes of sugary drinks, generally pushed from the left and resisted from the right. Such trivial conflicts presaged the emergence of much more serious political divisions around the response to the COVID-19 pandemic. Broadly speaking, the left has tended to champion the use of any means necessary in defence of health, where the right has tended to champion personal freedom against this.

The right-wing response thus tends to be reactionary in relation to the novel measures adopted by states to curb the spread of the virus. While 'freedom' serves as a convenient catch-all for objections to such state action, it is not always the normative basis for the right's opposition. Right-wing governments, in particular, have put the emphasis of their objections not on freedom but on simple economic prosperity. As discussed above, economic growth is a powerful norm for economic managers and the deliberate creation of a recession to protect public health powerfully contradicts the ideology of most politicians today, especially those of the right. Such an argument cannot find genuine popular purchase, however, since economic growth is an abstract concern not shared much by ordinary people. The point at which such a concern can be truly demotic is when it is posed as a question of whether people would rather be healthy or have a job. Being unemployed is almost as abnormal as being sick, and ordinary people risk their health all the time in order to have an income. At this level, it is a matter of a payoff not only between health and desire satisfaction, but also between health and basic material concerns like food and shelter that are themselves crucial to health. Relatedly, it is not entirely spurious when voices of the right suggest that health problems – principally mental illness – caused by lockdowns might outweigh the risk posed by the coronavirus, although most such commentary ignorantly fails to understand that the risk is posed less by the virus itself than by the possibility of the general burden on healthcare facilities overwhelming their capacity, leading to a cascading failure within the healthcare system. This is, on the opposite side, a relatively abstract concern that eludes the grasp of many minds.

Death

Contemporary medicine assesses the healthiness of practices in terms of associated morbidity and effects on longevity. For example, studies into the healthiness of coffee consumption try to determine the optimum number of coffees per day in terms of human lifespan. If people who have two coffees a day live longer than those who drink one or three, then two will be deemed the correct number to have. As I have suggested, of course, research never arrives at a final answer to such questions: different studies produce different answers, and new studies appear that contradict the old ones, seemingly without end.

In itself, living longer is a normative demand, ultimately implying a norm of eternal life. While we cannot yet say that it is normal to live forever (since, although complete compliance with norms is always impossible, something so apparently impossible cannot readily be posited explicitly), it's also not actually acknowledged that dying is normal. Of course almost everyone, if pushed, will agree that they must die, but I think there is a creeping doubt even about this because of technological progress, the dim or even fervent hope that technological advances will mean that *I* will be able to indefinitely defer the hour of my death, if only technology advances more quickly than my body declines. But even to accept death as inevitable is not the same as accepting it as normal, since that would imply it is also *desirable*. Death itself is thus abnormal, since its opposite – life – is the norm. And this implies that it must be considered both unnatural and unacceptable, even if it is hard to openly state as much – though Jean-Paul Sartre did write that 'It's not *natural* to die' as long ago as 1939.[6]

One exception to this antipathy towards death might seem to be the contemporary advocacy of legalizing 'euthanasia'. This might look like an attempt to establish proper norms for dying, and hence to normalize death. However, I believe it is really an attempt to deal with death in accordance with another norm, namely that we should never suffer (which is of course itself the inverse implication of the norm that we should always seek pleasure). Pain, like death, is considered generically abnormal, but eliminating pain is clearly more achievable – particularly if we are willing to choose death over pain.

The conflict here is once again effectively between the norms of life and of pleasure. Against euthanasia, it is sometimes asserted that it is good simply to remain alive, regardless of the quality of one's life. Now this does not quite seem to be the norm of 'health' as we have discussed it above, since people who are candidates for euthanasia are generally far from healthy, thus euthanasia may be presented as being in line with the norm of health, on the basis that if one cannot be made healthy, it is better one does not exist. However, the norm of health is, as discussed above, generally understood to involve longevity, with remaining alive an objective baseline indicator of health: our conception of health is tied to the norm of life. This is confused somewhat by the fact that many health advocates in fact push a fused message that is simultaneously about biological health and enjoyment, united around a *feeling* that healthiness is supposed to bring. This surely is simply the cost of doing business in a hedonistic society.

So, against the norm that it is good simply to remain alive, it is commonly inveighed that it is more desirable to die than to live a life dominated by the experience of pain. This is perfectly logical inasmuch as, today, although we hope for eternal life, we do so only on the basis that the value of life is in enjoying it. If my life cannot be made enjoyable, it may be seen as being without value.

This logic around euthanasia, that we should die if we can't live in accordance with the norm, is a particular case of the way the society of the norm pushes all of us, given the impossibility of meeting our targets, to consider suicide. This is not to say that there is nothing else motivating people to choose to die, of course. The desperation of someone with a severe degenerative illness – or indeed someone who is depressed or meets with frustrations – is not to be underestimated or reduced to the operation of norms: suicide is hardly a modern invention. My point is rather that norms push us further in this direction, even though suicide itself might be considered abnormal (although even this cannot be presumed to discourage suicide and might indeed be thought to encourage it, inasmuch as, if suicide is abnormal, once one starts down the road of suicidal ideation, this inclination only confirms one's abnormality all the more, implying a familiar spiral of anxiety).

One might note that an apparently quite different concept is often invoked by advocates of euthanasia, namely that of 'dignity', though what is considered 'dignified' here refers back to other norms, since really the 'indignities' suffered by the dying end up being things such as suffering, incapacity and, indeed, mere unaesthetic appearance, which indeed might be said to be unaesthetic precisely because it indicates suffering or the possibility of death itself. This last point is crucial: since dying is abnormal, any patina of death in life is considered inappropriate, as is any form of unhealthiness, to the point where we perhaps prefer someone to be dead than to be visibly *dying*. Certainly, we are a society that has banished the appearance of actual dead bodies. Rather, we are meant to die as healthily and happily as possible; advocates of euthanasia typically propose that we die with a surge of opiate-induced pleasure in which we indeed feel good, even as we die.

Artifice

The dream of abolishing death thus threatens to yield in the face of a more achievable aim of abolishing pain. But is there any prospect of pain actually being abolished? It is not clear to me that it is in prospect at all. Even if we could genetically edit someone such that they had no pain receptors, I do not believe we would do so, not least because it is considered normal to have the *capacity* to feel pain in appropriate situations, for it to hurt if we drop something on our foot, for example. We are aware that abolishing all such sensation of pain would be dangerous to our health. The norm of painlessness pushes not so much towards abolishing the physiological capacity for pain as towards abolishing the very contexts in which pain is normal. It's a matter not of preventing it from hurting when something falls on your foot so much as making sure nothing ever actually falls on anyone's foot. This indeed pushes in the direction of the avoidance of all danger, hence today's ever-burgeoning health-and-safety culture. But of course this cannot really eliminate suffering entirely.

The active dream of eliminating suffering altogether is perhaps most obviously encountered in transhumanism, a movement to use technology to change human capacities beyond their contemporary limitations, either through enhancing the physical body or by transcending it altogether in favour of a virtual existence. The transhumanist philosopher David Pearce has both predicted and advocated this.[7]

Transhumanism itself is decidedly weird, though. It violates basic norms. It is normal just to be human, not to transcend the human condition. However, I think that, paradoxically, just as death might seem preferable to an imperfect life, being disembodied might rate as less (definitely) abnormal than having an imperfect body, as a fortiori might enhancing one's body. Indeed, given that all bodies must be imperfect, the abolition of the body might be seen as a way to rid ourselves of this imperfection. Thus, we find ourselves effectively caught between the weirdness of having a body that we regard as abnormal and the weirdness of the imagined transcendence of that form. But the lure of transcending the body altogether is severely limited by its speculative nature and the extent to which the disembodied existence it posits cannot be said to be a continuation of the individuality that we so prize today. In any case, since our current norm of what it is to be human involves having a body, few would be willing to upload their mind out of their body unless that body were already on the verge of death.

What about the more realistic prospect of technological enhancements to the existing human body? Today, for the most part, people make changes to their bodies in order to attain a normal body. This is certainly the case for the primary use of prostheses, viz. to correct for 'disfigurement' or 'disabilities'. Prostheses are typically designed to restore a normal body and not, for example, to produce a body with capacities beyond those of the normal (which is to say able-bodied) human. Since the current image of what the body should be is never attained, however, there is in principle an open-ended possibility of enhancing any body in the direction of making it more normal. This fact might go some way towards explaining the runaway contemporary trend for modifying bodies superficially in the service of cosmetic outcomes. This mostly either occurs in pursuit of norms of physical appearance (in the case of cosmetic surgery) or consists in trivial cosmetic modification associated with fashion, in particular tattooing and piercing. It is unclear to me to what extent any norm is in fact in play in the latter set of fashions.[8] While there used to be norms that prohibited tattooing (or regulated it such that it was normal only for specific subsets of people who lived on the margins of Western society), these have clearly disappeared to a large extent. Indeed, it's quite possible that tattooing in younger generations has become not only normal but the norm in the sense that it is abnormal to have no tattoo. This is, then, a typical case of a new normal to which people conform because of its paradoxical potential for individualization, as well as its transgression of older, largely obsolete norms.

The normative bind in relation to body modification is that we are not only expected to have perfect bodies, but to do so naturally. Surgically enhanced bodies might seem more normal from a certain point of view, but having been modified makes them *ipso facto* abnormal. In cases where people are initially severely physically abnormal, there will be a higher relative normative impetus for surgical interventions. As normality is approached, however, the relative abnormality of being obviously surgically altered tends to outweigh any gain. I would suggest this is one reason for the well-known phenomenon of 'plastic surgery disasters', in which people continually alter their appearance in pursuit of an ideal but make themselves ultimately visibly more abnormal in the process.

I have suggested in relation to gender and sexuality that the notion of 'naturalness' can be deployed in the service of quite opposite norms, and to an extent this is true here too. Those who advocate enhancement of the human body may talk about unleashing its 'natural' potential. However, there is also a prominent sense in which 'naturalness' is invoked as something like the antonym of 'artificiality', that is, to refer to a refusal of technological fixes. And I would argue that this notion of 'naturalness' constitutes a major contemporary norm. Thus, for the moment, the use of prostheses to augment the human body such that it has increased capacities – like eugenics and genetic engineering for similar purposes – will remain marginal, and, indeed, largely taboo and illegal.

The significance of this valuation of naturalness as opposed to artificiality lies ultimately in the fact that all norms today are supposed to be met spontaneously without effort. Having to work at meeting norms marks the subject as abnormal, for if we were truly normal we would never have to do anything to be normal. Even if we become (relatively) normal through some process, this history of striving to meet the norm is a kind of stain of abnormality that will haunt it.

An attempt to deal with the inevitable difficulties this brings is found in the enthusiasm for *natural* remedies, for example in the prominent, popular and diverse discourse of 'natural health' that prefers plant extracts to synthesized medications. Such interventions are presented as merely 'restoring' a natural state, 'detoxifying' us, rather than altering us artificially: the natural cure is supposed merely to bring out our natural essence, and hence frees us from any idea that we were ever intrinsically abnormal.

The claims of natural health frequently run contrary to the norms of knowledge production in medical science. It finds popularity among masses of people over whom the epistemological norm of empiricism has no particular hold. However, for all its apparent anti-modernism, advocates of natural health seek ultimately to realize the same contemporary health norms of longevity and painlessness as conventional medicine does. One sees this dynamic in relation to childbirth, for example: so-called 'natural childbirth' ultimately follows the same norms as artificial birthing practices, inasmuch as both follow the norm that life should be preserved and the birthing process painless. Whereas giving birth in a conventional hospital may be rendered comfortable with drugs, natural birth advocates believe that it will be essentially painless if we do everything entirely naturally. I'm sure, of course, that natural birth advocates also do say that giving birth will always involve *some* pain – just as advocates of conventional obstetrics do – but then, since everything in life involves some pain, this is not much of a concession, and they can still hold that there will be less pain than in even heavily drugged hospital deliveries. This is unfalsifiable: since natural childbirth is an asymptote, we can always say that there is some way that any actual, painful birth has fallen short of full naturalness, and that thus it is the non-natural element that is to blame for the pain.

6

Law

In this chapter I will consider the figurative and literal 'pointy end' of norms and normalization: their enforcement. I will discuss two different dimensions of this: its obvious instantiation in the judicial system, as well as the most direct application of the logic of normalization to human behaviour, psychology.

Guilty

For Foucault, the law is in a peculiar position in relation to norms. On the one hand, it is, in a sense, the main rival to the norm. The law was the main way in which society was regulated prior to the rise of the norm, hence the thing that norms most displace, and therefore the main basis for resistance to the normalizing society as it emerged. On the other hand, in the society of the norm, the law, like everything else, must be subordinated to the model of the norm.

Foucault says – unfortunately without explaining what he means – that the law has come to function more and more like a norm.[1] To say that the law itself has become a norm is to imply that it is operating not merely *in pursuit of* an unattainable vision of perfection (as we would expect to the extent it has been subordinated to norms), but that it has itself become an ideal of perfection in pursuit of which other things are done. This implies that the law no longer functions as a set of rules but has come to operate also as a nebulous standard for behaviour with which no one is ever in accordance and in relation to which one can hence always be normalized. My interpretation of this is that the extraordinary growth in the number and complexity of laws has meant that the law no longer operates a discrete code but instead as precisely a nebulous norm to which nothing ever completely conforms.

There has always been a palpable disconnect between the letter and the operation of the law: the law relies constitutively on a pretension to fairness, but in practice has always been applied at least somewhat corruptly and arbitrarily. Nonetheless, the law itself has comprised a discrete set of rules to which people were supposed in principle to conform. This remains its putative model. The number and complexity of laws has, however, increased enormously – even exponentially – in recent times. This inflation in the size of the statute books means that the law has become a nebulous standard that cannot be met: no one can any longer claim to know the entirety of the legal code, and indeed no one can even say at the federal level in the United States, for example, exactly how many enforceable laws exist,[2] which surely precludes the possibility of strict compliance with all applicable laws at all times.

What this means is that, in relation to the law, as in relation to medicine, today, whether one is institutionally normalized or not is primarily a question of whether resources are brought to bear and to what end. By the very nature of norms, there is no defined point at which behaviour becomes abnormal, hence institutional normalization is always Kafkaesque. To be sure, the application of the law has always been arbitrary; what is different now is the mechanism by which the law is arbitrarily applied, no longer only by manufacturing evidence, bribery and other forms of obvious corruption, but more and more by the technical manipulation of the law's own indeterminateness.

As a concrete example of what I mean here, I would adduce the case of Khalifah Al-Akili, an American Muslim.[3] The FBI poured resources into pursuing Al-Akili for suspected terrorism. When their surveillance came to nought, they raided his home. There, they discovered video footage showing him firing a gun at a firing range. As a previously convicted felon, Al-Akili was banned from possessing firearms, so even for him to pick up a gun was technically a crime. He was sentenced to ninety-four months in gaol on the basis of a few seconds of video, even though there was no evidence any of this had any connection to terrorism. Had he not been prosecuted for this infraction, doubtless some more minor offence, from a driving infraction to an irregularity with his taxes, could have been found. It is also possible the authorities might concoct evidence of a nonexistent crime, but my point is that every individual will have broken some law at some point, knowingly or unknowingly, which can be discovered given enough surveillance of them and enough mining of the statute books. We are all criminals – that is, all abnormal in relation to the norm provided by the law – and whether we are convicted of a crime is ultimately a question of the state's willingness to pursue us.

There is a converse to this, namely that it is possible to escape almost any prosecution by exploiting the nebulous standard of evidence and procedural norms. For one thing, in modern common law jurisprudence, the standard of evidence is that criminality be proven 'beyond reasonable doubt'; with sufficient resources, one may find a way to cast doubt on any defendant's guilt. The OJ Simpson trial is perhaps the most famous example of this. There is also simply the possibility of using the ubiquitousness of violations of the law against prosecutions: if everyone violates the law at some point, this is also true of the agents of law enforcement themselves, a fact that can be uncovered with sufficient investigative resources and then provide the basis for declaring an entire case void (an effort in this direction was another major tactic of the Simpson defence). Moreover, given the nebulous expanse of the law, with enough resources one can always find legal loopholes. We can here point to the exploitation of forms of insanity defence by wealthy defendants, such as the 2013 'affluenza' defence of Texan teenager Ethan Couch after he killed four people, which argued that the defendant's family's wealth had rendered him incapable of taking personal responsibility.[4] The nebulousness of psychological norms that allow anyone to be diagnosed as mentally ill means that such a diagnosis can ultimately be concocted in relation to any criminal charges. In the end, then, the law, much like psychology, and sometimes through psychology, is subject to binary gatekeeping based on the means of those concerned, because it is a norm that no one actually meets. Any normalizing institution, be it the juridical system, psychiatry or physical healthcare, can and will categorize anyone as abnormal – be it in the form of having committed a crime or of having some illness – if sufficient resources are brought to bear on analysing that individual. This is not to say, of course, that such resources are always, or even often, brought to bear.

The same pattern is, in effect, found informally in contemporary 'cancel culture', as illustrated by the 'milkshake duck' meme, which originated in a tweet by Australian cartoonist Ben Ward telling the brief story of a duck that is famous for loving milkshakes, but is later revealed to be racist. This refers to the phenomenon of short-lived internet sensations who are specifically later revealed to have 'problematic' opinions. It alludes perhaps most clearly to Ken Bone, a member of the public who asked a question in a 2016 televised US presidential debate that led to widespread and ubiquitous admiration, followed by the revelation that he had, as Vox put it, 'a seriously sketchy Reddit comment history'.[5] This phenomenon of the inevitability that anyone exposed to public scrutiny will be found in some way 'problematic' seems to me to be a simple consequence of the inevitable violation of social norms by every individual (the same effect observed in relation to the 'having a normal one' trope discussed earlier in the book). If we allow ad hominem condemnations on the basis of a given individual's abnormal behaviour – as we apparently now do – this weapon can be turned against anyone at any time for any purpose, depending ultimately only on the willingness of people and the media to propagate this cancellation in relation to that individual.

Sin

This ubiquitousness of the violation of norms implies a pervasive feeling of guilt: to the extent that we are aware of the existence of any norm (and I have suggested we must be aware of this – consciously or unconsciously – to a large extent), we must feel guilty in relation to it, and we inevitably to some extent will violate every norm of which we are aware.

As I have said already, this guilt is ubiquitous in a different way from that implied by the Christian concept of sin. While the Christian worldview holds people responsible for their sins and requires atonement, it does not traditionally allow the possibility of ever actually achieving sinlessness. Rather, we are expected only to beg forgiveness for our sinfulness. While it is a precondition of forgiveness that we make some attempt not to sin, failure in this regard is understood as inevitable.[6]

The society of the norm, by contrast, lacks any central agency akin either to the Church or to God, and can therefore offer no redemption through forgiveness, convincing people in effect that they are alone in their abnormality, that most people somehow are not abnormal, and that, if they are, they simply must rid themselves of their abnormality, even though this is impossible and, indeed, at a certain level this impossibility must be manifest to everyone.

This is not to say there is no connection between the Christian concept of sin and the modern concept of abnormality. We can understand abnormality as a kind of secularized version of the concept of sin, replacing that notion now that we have increasingly lost our religious faith. I want to suggest, however, that – contrary to popular doxa regarding Christianity today – the Christian notion of sin implies *less* guilt than the secular notion of abnormality.

The new society of the norm presents itself as a release from guilt: it says that you do not need to be beholden to the old Christian morality, that you can do whatever you want. As Lacan put it, however, if God does not exist, everything is forbidden.[7] Lacan's point is that, without the old limits to structure our desires, it becomes impossible to desire anything. My core point here is related, but different: namely that, without a structure of discrete moral guidelines, we are exposed to the full force of absolute norms that demand perfection – which forbids everything short of perfection, that is, everything that can ever actually exist. Although we could never fully be in accordance with the morality of Christianity, could never be fully Christ-like and without sin, we could prostrate ourselves before the absolute represented by God and seek forgiveness via a relation with an actualized perfection. Without a religion through which to approach the absolute, we stand naked before it, like the men exposed directly to the raw stuff of God at the denouement of *Raiders of the Lost Ark*, their faces melting. Less metaphorically, without a belief in the absolute, we have no choice but to try to become the absolute ourselves in order to fill this void. This is what norms ultimately enjoin. To become the absolute – to become God – is a task that we are surely not up to. How can we cope with this impossible injunction? For Christians, it was in an eventual unity with God (or at least resurrection in His kingdom) that perfection would be attained, not in this life. For secular moderns, this life is all there is, so we either achieve perfection here or die trying. One solution is to try to convince ourselves that we have already reached perfection. In a sense, today, we all believe we are perfect already, since we are without sin – but then this leaves us chronically unable to explain why we are evidently lacking in perfections. Denial and even psychotic delusion are, as Freud says, never a successful strategy because even the psychotic is at some level aware that they are delusional.[8]

Christianity in the age of the norm has itself accordingly become an altered beast. In contemporary Protestantism, in particular, some denominations hold that people can become sinless thereby removing the structures of penance and contrition that previously allowed people to feel better, a tendency that began most obviously in John Wesley's eighteenth-century Christian 'perfectionism'. There has been a general tendency for the ethos of Christianity to transform into a blithe positivity, emphasizing love and acceptance over depravity and contrition. This process is far from uniform or complete, but it has made religion less apt to protect believers from absolutization.

Psych-

Care for the soul has now in general passed from religion to medicine. This has been accomplished through an ambiguous shift to speaking in terms of the 'mind' or 'psyche' instead of the 'soul', and then by identifying this 'mind' with a bodily organ, the brain, which we increasingly substitute for 'mind' in our speech. These moves allow the human being to be medically normalized not only in action but also in thought, by conceptually assimilating the soul to the body.

We have seen how the diffusion of medical notions of normality has given rise to problematic social expectations. In general, however, there does not seem to be any route to obviating this if we are to retain the heuristic of normality within medicine, which seems to be necessary for it to function as well as it does. Still, there are particular areas of medical normalization that are far more concerned than others with fostering social expectations and less with the needs of physical health. I am thinking specifically of psychiatry and psychology. In these disciplines, unlike in core areas of medicine, it is not merely the human body and its functioning that is deemed to be either normal or abnormal, but rather human behaviour and human thought.

The key conceptual move for the medicalization of the mind is the notion of mental *illness*, which is to say, strictly speaking, the idea that certain *thoughts* can be indicative of – or simply are in themselves – sick. Although the exact phrase 'mental illness' is actually a twentieth-century invention, this process of the normalizing pathologization of thought began early in the nineteenth century, if not before.

While psychology and psychiatry are supposedly concerned with the mind, their real focus is on *behaviour*, for the unavoidable reason that these disciplines have yet to gain direct access to patients' consciousnesses. Doctors and psychologists must therefore make inferences from patients' observable behaviour – including their speech as a privileged window into the soul – to an underlying abnormality of the mind. The more technical vocabulary of these fields is not one of mental 'illness' but precisely of mental 'disorder' – or, indeed, explicitly of behavioural disorder.

The diagnosis of behavioural symptoms can be addressed by investigations into whether there might be organic causes, in particular investigations into whether there are underlying neurological issues, and also questions of genetic or ordinary physiological causes. Where these are located, it is determined that the illness is not finally psychiatric, and thus that it falls within the remit of a different branch of medicine. Despite the fact that psychology and psychiatry intervene in cases where organic causes cannot readily be found, however, their dominant approach today is one that assumes that mental illness must ultimately be physical in nature and therefore attempts to cure it by physical means. Although medicine has taken control of the mental by declaring it to be essentially neurological, despite massive ongoing efforts, the mental stubbornly remains as an area that cannot be explained or treated simply by organic interventions of the type that medicine typically traffics in.

The approach to mental 'health' today is caught in a physicalism closely aligned with its incorporation into medicine. The first resort in psychological care is crudely physical: we are enjoined to take regular exercise, to eat healthily, to sleep more and to engage in wholesome activities, such as social pastimes, and perhaps to take a holiday. Essentially, when people have behavioural problems, the first recourse of medics is to tell them to stop behaving abnormally. The next step is to move on to address apparently abnormal thoughts, which are understood as 'cognitive behaviour', and are corrected by telling patients to stop thinking in this way, which is what so-called 'cognitive behavioural therapy', the dominant contemporary modality of psychotherapy, actually amounts to. This tactic of telling people to stop thinking abnormally is really the only specifically psychological weapon the mainstream of contemporary psychology has in its armoury, as witnessed in more or less every single episode of the US talk show *Dr. Phil*, in which the psychologist host inevitably ends up telling the guests that only they can change themselves and that he is helpless in the face of their inability or unwillingness to do so.

Off-screen, if a patient persists in bad thoughts or deeds, the psychologist's next intervention is to drug them – and frequently the drugs come from a medic before the patient is ever sent for psychological counselling. If lifestyle changes don't improve the thoughts, or if the patient cannot or will not change their lifestyle, then it is inferred that there must be an underlying 'chemical imbalance' in their brain, to be treated with pharmaceuticals that correct it at a neurochemical level – even though no actual neurological condition can be identified as such.

How does one determine whether there is a disorder to be treated in the first place? Worldwide, psychologists and psychiatrists use the *Diagnostic and Statistical Manual* (*DSM*), compiled under the auspices of the American Psychological Association, a gazetteer of psychological disorders. There is no one-to-one correlation between singular behaviours and the disorders listed in this publication, however. It rather deems a *pattern* of behaviour to amount to a disorder. It posits no underlying reality behind this pattern. That is to say, disorders are not understood as distinct mental *or* physical states. 'Disorder' is, rather, effectively an assessment of the behaviour itself as disordered. Compare this to the psychoanalytical approaches that dominated psychiatry and psychology in the mid-twentieth century, which actually drew inferences from behaviour and speech to obscure objects in the unconscious mind. Psychoanalysis thus posited disorders not as behavioural but as internal conditions of the mind itself, as a *sui generis* object. Psychoanalysis has never entirely disappeared from psychiatry and psychology, but is today a highly marginal school of thought in them, at least in the English-speaking world.

The very idea of a mental 'disorder' implies that there is a correct (or normal) order for the psyche. The *DSM* sets out no positive standard for normal behaviour, however – indeed, the very existence of such a norm is only negatively implied. This is unavoidable for psychology, inasmuch as, where body temperature is measured objectively against an admittedly arbitrary standard, behaviour cannot be measured objectively at all. The *DSM* instead relies on profoundly subjective clinical judgements in its application. Its categories are (perhaps unavoidably) described in such elastic terms that there is almost unlimited scope to fit people into whatever category a clinician is minded to put them. Indeed, it is not clear that there is any human behaviour that cannot be deemed abnormal according to the *DSM*, or any human being who cannot be diagnosed with some or other mental illness thereby. While I cannot possibly prove this, since one cannot prove a negative, I do not believe that there is anyone who could not ultimately be categorized under the *DSM* where the clinical will exists to do so. The fact that most people are not categorized as mentally ill today amounts, on this view, to the fact that no clinician has ever made an active effort to categorize them as mentally ill. This situation may change in the future as more and more people actively seek, or are referred to, psychological professionals.

Psychonosography thus resembles the contemporary law, providing guidelines vague enough that any individual can be diagnosed with some or other disorder by a clinician seeking to diagnose them, a point to which I will return in more detail below. The lack of a positive description of the norm is thus not exceptional in this case, but precisely how norms tend to operate. Something similar is true also of physiological medicine: if there is sufficient will to find someone ill, a malady will be found, not in this case so much because the normative parameters are not objective (though in some areas of organic medicine this may also be the case), but because of the omnipresence of minute variations from perfectly normal organic function. Indeed, given that psychiatry is a branch of medicine, it is itself implicated here: if someone complains they are physically ill but is deemed to be physically healthy, then they have a mental illness, viz. hypochondria – or else can be supposed to have an undetectable physical malady.

Since psychiatry and psychology diagnose on the basis of patients' behaviour, they essentially seek to effect changes in behaviour. That is, it is behaviour that they ultimately seek to normalize. In this they constitute one side of a reversible coin of behavioural normalization, with criminal law providing the other. Any behaviour may be disciplined either by psychology or by the law, or indeed by both simultaneously. Foucault details how, historically, those deemed criminal and insane were, at one time, indifferently confined along with the destitute in a single institution of confinement, before differential institutions – the prison and the asylum, respectively – developed to separate those deemed to be criminally culpable from the insane and from the poor.[9] This led to a situation where, at the point of trial, anyone can be declared incompetent by reason of insanity and treated psychologically for their criminal behaviour, instead of facing criminal sanctions. Given what I have said about the universal possibilities of determining any individual to be either mentally deficient or a criminal, the category one is deemed to belong to here must always be somewhat arbitrary. Of course, there are cases in which the behaviour of an accused seems more indicative of mental disturbance than in others, hence some cases lend themselves more to a finding of reduced culpability. However, this is also surely at least somewhat dependent on the quality of one's counsel and expert witnesses, as well as a series of arbitrary prejudices about what behaviours the mentally

Law

disturbed engage in. Any adverse behaviour could be described as a psychological disorder, so criminal behaviour is always ripe for psychological categorization and treatment. Conversely, the behaviours of the mentally 'ill' are often likely to be transgressive in ways that attract the intervention of law enforcement, and any mentally ill person (just like any other person) can be targeted to be dragged before the courts. It follows that the status both of being mentally ill and of being a criminal are effectively reversible, although they are also far from mutually exclusive.

In the past half century, we have seen a change in the balance of power between psychology and jurisprudence occasioned by the wholesale closure of the asylums that were once the principal way of dealing with those deemed insane, and, a fortiori, those deemed criminally so. The explicit logic of this closure was that such confinement of the insane was inhumane and ineffective. This logic, however, has not yet been allowed to seriously trouble the prison system, which is similarly demonstrably both inhuman and ineffective – indeed, imprisonment has increased to levels never before seen in human history, particularly in the United States, notwithstanding certain recent moves in the opposite direction and the sudden popularization of the cause of prison abolition. This difference is surely due to the fact that prisoners are held to be morally culpable for their criminality, whereas patients in psychiatric institutions were generically understood to be blameless. Another factor is the appearance of effective new behavioural modifiers in the form of new generations of psychoactive medications that could be offered outside the asylum setting, whereas there was no equivalent development in the evolution of the punishment of criminals (although perhaps the use of electronic monitoring echoes it weakly). This post-asylum approach to disciplining psychological abnormality, called 'care in the community' in the UK, is not marked by greater effectiveness, but it is significantly cheaper to administer. A major side effect of this approach, though, is that those who cannot be contained easily in the community tend, in the absence of asylums, to be imprisoned instead.[10] Indicating the continuing reversibility between the jurisprudential and the psychological, prison inmates, on the other hand, are increasingly diagnosed with mental disorders and placated through psychoactive medications.[11]

The absence of hard disciplinary controls on mental patients has made them largely responsible for their own care. This of course appears to bring them a measure of freedom, but it does so precisely by making them internalize the normative framework of psycho-nosography. Patients increasingly identify with their diagnoses: in an era in which we seek our authentic natures, all medical diagnoses are apt to be treated by the diagnosed as revelations of their true essences. This is perhaps particularly the case in relation to psychiatric diagnoses, since these are peculiarly apt to seem to tell us who we are at a deep level, describing not merely our organic characteristics but our personalities. Today we witness the appearance of something like identitarian movements around such diagnoses – for example, by those on what is now called the 'autism spectrum', and also people with anxiety disorders, depressive disorders, bipolar disorder, borderline personalities, etc., forming 'communities', particularly online. Such diagnoses can be liberating for subjects to the extent that they explain their nonconformity with prevailing norms, but I would argue this cannot offer a strategy for liberation because it simultaneously involves a definitive self-assumption of abnormality (hence a permanent, if different, feeling of disease), while also applying a label that inevitably brings with it its own normative expectations.

Psychonosography is profoundly complicit in this development. While the *DSM* is notionally a merely nosographic guide, without supposed ontological claims about the reality of the conditions it describes, the diagnostic methodology it implies relies not only on subjective judgements of those who diagnose; it also accepts as accurate patients' subjective reports about their own affects and thoughts. This at least opens the door to patients to influence their own diagnosis.

Against such practices, I would again counterpose the depth psychology of psychoanalysis, which attempts to infer and to uncover structures beyond the patient's awareness and initial descriptions. More particularly, I would champion the Lacanian variety of psychoanalysis, which no longer traffics in psychopathology, but simply sees everyone as having different structural problems, with no unproblematic normal state being posited as a normative guide. The Lacanian analyst, moreover, does not propose diagnoses 'analysand' (rather than 'patient') – if the analyst makes such judgements, they do not generally inform the analysand of these – but, rather, mentors them in a journey of self-understanding. Lacanian psychoanalysis thus actively assumes the role of helping people produce a narrative about themselves, without directing it.

Lacanians do not deny that there are states of mind that people find to be deleterious to themselves, nor do they seek to invalidate anyone's desire to change their mentality to avoid these; indeed, they seek to help analysands in this regard. One could even say that, on Canguilhem's model of medical normality, if anyone thinks their thoughts are abnormal, then they must indeed be so. What I am rejecting is the contemporary approach that seeks to normalize people based on supposedly objective norms of human behaviour. This illusory norm is, I would argue, in itself apt to provoke or at least exacerbate what is called mental illness.

Perfectionism

The society of the norm as I have described it implies a pervasive culture of what might be called 'perfectionism', an absolute demand for perfection in all arenas. The attempts by psychology to identify and deal with the existence of perfectionism in our society show the difficulties inherent in its operation in a normalizing society. Psychology is tasked, in effect, with dealing with the consequences of normalization, but is also perhaps the strongest single vector of contemporary normalization, so it is tasked with curing what it is, at the same time, causing.

For contemporary psychology, 'perfectionism' figures not as a disorder in its own right, but as a symptom that might indicate a psychological disorder. The psychology literature distinguishes three dimensions of perfectionism: 'self-oriented', 'other-oriented' and 'socially prescribed'.[12] Really, however, these varieties are all aspects of a single phenomenon. All our ideals are always related to ourselves, to others and to society. While there may be a difference in the degree to which we believe our ideals are prescribed by the society around us, they surely always derive from it. Conversely, I would suggest, it is difficult to hold ourselves to a high standard without somehow applying this standard also to those around us, or vice versa. Christianity does enjoin this (forgive others' trespasses, seek forgiveness for our trespasses), but in our narcissistic culture we instead tend towards a spiralling cycle of recrimination alternating between ourselves and other people. Some people clearly are not inclined to be self-critical but seem only to criticize others instead, but in such cases we can say that hostility towards others is always in a sense self-directed as well as vice versa: when we criticize others, this always indicates a lack of self-confidence, in the same way that failing to criticize others while criticizing oneself might also betoken a similar lack, and indeed a certain implicit hostility to others.

Shorn of these dubious directional distinctions, the psychological account of perfectionism amounts to saying that some people engage in unwarranted criticism of themselves and others that makes them unhappy. This implies that most people don't do this and that a 'normal' person criticizes themselves and others only when it is warranted. I would suggest that this image of a normal, nonperfectionist criticizer is unachievable in a society of the norm. Of course, inasmuch as this image is itself a norm, we should expect it to be unachievable, but the unachievability of this particular norm is a kind of meta case, since it depends on the unachievability of all other norms. Whether or not people are deemed deserving of criticism is itself relative to the norms that obtain in any area of life; by the nature of norms, this means criticism in relation to them will always to some extent be seen as justified. That is to say that almost everyone today is really, increasingly, a 'perfectionist', and liable to be deemed so.[13] In the case of a high-functioning perfectionist whose perfectionism inspires them to great achievements such that they feel relatively satisfied, a psychologist will likely look at them and say that there is no problem. Someone with the same ideals who is less capable of achieving them, however, might be regarded as sick because their perfectionism makes them anxious and self-hating. The difference would be extrinsic rather than inherent in the patients.

Implying that perfectionism is abnormal in a society in which it is ubiquitous is tantamount to mass gaslighting: the contemporary perfectionist is told that they are bad not only for failing to reach the image of perfection that society provides for them, but also for holding themselves to this standard, even though the standard is outside their control. It is a high irony that psychologists criticize perfectionism in the service of a norm which itself amounts to a vision of perfect human behaviour.

Of course, the quest for perfection never appears in an entirely unadulterated state. It is never the sole motivation and content of any human activity. For example, people do not work out solely to attain the perfect healthy and sculpted body. They also do it because exercise is addictive, and indeed this addiction may cause people to work out beyond the point at which it is healthy. Yet it is also true that no one manifested this particular addiction in pre-modern societies, whatever contemporary advocates of a 'Bronze Age mindset' might claim.[14]

Doesn't my critique here itself amount to a norm that casts perfectionism as abnormal? I would say not, inasmuch as my overarching point is that we can criticize things without counterposing an alternative vision that we consider superior, which is to say, without a norm. I think it would be good if we could be less perfectionist, but do not want to establish any norm of anti-perfectionist perfection.

Divergence

In closing this chapter, I want to acknowledge that, in the past few years, a new term, 'neurodivergence' seems abruptly to have replaced 'mental illness' as the preferred way of describing behavioural abnormality, with the term 'neurotypical' being used to describe the behaviourally normal. This new vocabulary interestingly points in two distinct directions: it doubles down on the physicalism and statisticalism of the understanding of abnormal behaviour, while suddenly refusing its medicalization. That is to say, it reduces the mental to the neural, while at the same time refusing to categorize abnormal behaviour as sick, but rather only as atypical.

On the one hand, this refusal is akin – or even directly related – to that seen in the rejection of the psychiatrization of being transgender. Neurodivergence is not presented as something curable, precisely because it is neural rather than mental, thus inherent, although this does not mean that medicine does not have palliatives to offer, that is, the appropriate drugs to shape the experience of whichever particular divergence one might exhibit, much as medicine can offer gender reassignment to trans people.

On the other hand, this way of speaking elevates everyone's difference by declaring difference to be unusual. Most people clearly diverge from any norm of behaviour, but describing this as 'divergence' from a 'typical' obfuscates this fact and allows everyone's unique psychology to be valorized as such. The assertion of neurodivergence is effectively a way to normalize mental illness – since divergence is *ipso facto* normal in our *soi-disant* diverse society – albeit on a false basis.

7

Difference

Today we laud difference. This means we consider it normal to be different, but also more than this: today, if you are not different, you are considered abnormal. If there is one thing that encapsulates the mutation of normality over the past half century or so and the paradoxical form it has assumed, it is precisely this: everyone has to be absolutely the same in being absolutely different, which is to say absolutely individual. Trivially, since we are all different from one another and are all individuals, we always already have some basis on which to conform to this norm. But qua norm, the principle of difference elevates individuality to an absolute standard that is impossible for anyone to meet.

Two of the three most prominent French philosophers of the late twentieth century, Gilles Deleuze and Jacques Derrida, articulated philosophies of difference that rejected identity and sameness (albeit in quite distinct ways). The somewhat younger French philosopher, Alain Badiou, perhaps the most significant thinker of his own generation, has pointed out in reaction the extent to which mere difference cannot ground anything, but

Difference

rather there must be some positing of *sameness* in order to generate meaning.[1]

The elevation of difference is supposed, of course, to shatter norms, but it does not do so. Paradoxically, these philosophies that supposedly oppose binaries in the name of difference actually end up establishing a binary normative drama in which assertions of sameness and identity in the face of difference are considered evil.

Whatever the intentions of the philosophers of difference, clearly not all differences are considered equal in our society. Since some characteristics are considered normal and others abnormal, to be different in the direction of abnormality is reckoned to be bad. The rhetoric of difference might be deployed to defend abnormality by saying that, while someone might be mentally ill, or indeed even criminal or violent, they are merely expressing their own individuality. Such a rhetorical strategy effectively amounts to pointing out that someone is in accordance with the norm of difference, but this will not be enough to excuse that person's violation of other norms – at most, it may distract attention away from normative violations for a time.

Diversity

Thus, certain differences remain decisively abnormal, even as difference in general has been elevated to a normative principle. The radical change brought by the normalization of difference as such is that what previously was considered archetypically normal, namely sameness, is now considered abnormal, and vice versa. This newly abnormal category consists of the characteristics that were the marks of conformity in the preceding

Difference

normative order. They are, namely, the familiar raft of whiteness, heterosexuality, maleness, cis-genderedness, etc. These older normative characteristics are those against which a new norm of *diversity* has been constitutively defined.

The norm of diversity was initially applied specifically to groups. In the case of any given group, the question could be asked whether it was sufficiently diverse. If it was not, it could be diversified by increasing the representation of underrepresented categories of people, be they minority ethnicities, women or those with non-heterosexual sexualities. The negative corollary of this has been a tendential fight against normative homogeneity of whiteness, maleness, heterosexuality, etc. Consistent with the pragmatics of this enterprise, we find homogeneously black or female groups celebrated as 'diverse', even though they are not literally inherently diverse in the ordinary sense of the word, but rather betoken a broader diversification. As a logic of the group, declaring *homogenous* whiteness, heterosexuality, cis-masculinity, etc. to be abnormal has had a clear aim of proactively preventing the exclusion of non-white, non-heterosexual, non-cis-males who have historically been quite deliberately excluded from important arenas.

A group can be diverse inherently, or it can become more diverse relative to the composition of similar groups. Yet, as a norm in an unprecedentedly individualistic society (one in which individuality is one of the most potent norms), the norm of diversity has unsurprisingly – and perhaps unavoidably – come to bear on the individual. Individuals are now described as personally, inherently, 'diverse' – I was in a meeting in 2020 in which a senior colleague positively described a young woman of colour as a 'diverse young woman'

Difference

– despite the fact that this is a corporate, not an individual, category, and one, moreover, that can only ever be a relative attribute. An individual cannot be diverse in any straightforward way, by contrast, unless it is in the trivial sense that all individuals are complex.

The status of the norm of diversity as a new norm for individuals is palpable in the reaction to a 2017 grassroots far-right social media campaign promoting the slogan 'It's okay to be white'. This slogan was deliberately crafted as a provocation, and was profoundly effective as such, producing exactly the reaction it predicted, namely that this apparently banal assertion was generally deemed unacceptable. This seems to imply that it is in fact *not* OK, not acceptable, to be white.

I have argued above that, in terms of the logic of the norm, whatever it is acceptable to do must be normal: for something to be normal does not make it one of an array of acceptable options, but rather establishes it as *normative*. This thus explains precisely why our society cannot allow that it is OK to be white: whiteness clearly used to be normative, but at this point our culture has in large part (though not yet entirely) forcefully rejected that norm. We genuinely cannot inveigh that it is 'okay' to be white without allowing that being white is normal. The difficulty of course is that saying it is normal to be white implies it is abnormal to be non-white.

Now, there is an obvious alternative here, that which has played out in relation to sexuality, which would be to have no norm in relation to colour/race at all. This gesture, normative 'colour-blindness', is widely opposed by the left because it would not prevent the rectifying elevation of non-white people. Unfortunately, in the terms of the discussion in this book, this amounts to asserting the exclusive normality of non-whiteness.

Difference

What needs to be understood, however, and is generally obscured because it is unpalatable to so many people, is that this necessarily means rendering whiteness a form of abnormality. And this, I think, has clearly happened, at least in certain circles, which happen to be culturally dominant in our society. It has become commonplace to deride whiteness in public and in polite company. It is normal at this point to declare that 'white people' are bad, to deride someone's whiteness where it is seen to be causally connected to another bad trait, such as denigrated political opinions or artistic tastes. It is also increasingly declared that white people have certain responsibilities incumbent on them to atone for their whiteness, without there being any clear prospect of any acts undertaken by individual whites in relation to 'decolonization' or 'allyship' actually definitively making their whiteness OK. It generates, rather, like all normative discourses, a never-ending failure that can only be acknowledged as such. This anti-white discourse is, I should perhaps note, often – and I think mostly – heard from white people themselves, having in no small part been pioneered by them.

We see here the playing out of a negation of older norms to hyperbolic extremes. The new normal is not simply the negation of the old norms, however, but is also a new norm in its own right, demanding that everyone be *perfectly* deviant from the old norm, which is impossible. The ambiguity of norms is such that, just as no one ever perfectly conformed to the old norms of whiteness, heterosexuality, maleness, etc., but could point to their broad conformity with some or other convention in order to fit in, every individual can now try to avoid castigation by pointing out something that mitigates their whiteness, heterosexuality, maleness, etc. However, every real individual can conversely also

Difference

be suspected of failing to conform to this new norm by embodying some form of whiteness (if not ethnic, then cultural, say), maleness, etc. One reason I suspect the new normal is so prevalent online is that its partisans can escape the normalizing gaze that might find them wanting by existing only as a disembodied negative voice of condemnation that it is hard to turn into a target – while any definite, real individual who is targeted can always be found to have some trace of privilege. The same thing may be said of the new normal's opposite online shadow world, the far-right online subculture, wherein anonymous contributors aggressively signal adherence to a mutant version of the old norms, with posters denouncing one another as being something other than white, straight, male, American, etc.

Such a reaction is as predictable as it is lamentable. The lauding of diversity as an inherent attribute that one either does or does not possess cannot but make the non-diverse subject feel abnormal, much as everyone who is *not* male, white, or cis-heterosexual has long been made to feel abnormal by the older norms. While whiteness and maleness, in particular, still correlate statistically to wealth, power and privilege in our society, they are now accompanied by a supplement of psychological anxiety. This anxiety is the inverse of the longstanding psychological effect of racism on non-white people in a society in which non-whites could never truly find acceptance. The contemporary situation is one in which this older racism continues, but where the privileged group (that is, whites) themselves also increasingly feel marginalized. A majority of white people in the United States report that they believe white people are discriminated against, for example.[2] This is not merely a paranoid fantasy on their part, but an unavoidable affective corollary of a genuine and concerted strategy

Difference

to fight white privilege through the normative elevation of divergence from the old norms. While one might say that whites deserve this marginalization, or that it is itself a minor inconvenience relative to white privilege, it is analytically necessary to note this effect if one wants to understand contemporary reactionary politics in the West. One effect is that discourses of the far right that were once paranoid fantasies now find more purchase in reality (although I should note that a more paranoid fantasy might be more politically successful than a less paranoid and fantastical political analysis). Whites feel themselves to be maligned, something that is seized on by extremists who demand that whites be recognized as a distinct minority group with sectional interests, even while whites are in the majority. It is far from obvious, as identitarians shrilly point out, what, in the contemporary discourse of diversity and difference, prevents them from claiming such rights, and indeed one of the more worrisome aspects of these norms is that, although they originate in the negation of older norms, they in fact provide a normative framework that is profoundly ambiguous in its future trajectory.

One banal fact underlying the pathetic reaction represented by white identity politics is that the contemporary norm makes whites feel that they must apologize for themselves, which is particularly uncomfortable for people unused to this requirement. A more disconcerting dimension, however, is that the maligning of a group will inevitably be felt most keenly by its least privileged members. While wealthier and more privileged whites can, with relative ease, materially bear and culturally navigate a discourse that casts whiteness as non-ideal, poorer whites have much less in their lives to console themselves when their skin colour, which was previously an asset to them, increasingly becomes a liability. Indeed, for poor whites, whiteness was a rare area in which they felt previously that they were able to conform with a norm. This is consonant with the fact that whites report experiencing more racial discrimination against them the lower their income level.[3]

Of course, non-whites can hardly be expected to shed tears for the fact that the poorest whites are now in a relatively similar position to poor people of colour. My point is not that they should, but rather that this norm-shifting does almost nothing to seriously disturb the privilege of the most privileged whites, who are in compliance with a plethora of norms, and who can easily camouflage themselves with diversity in various regards, particularly by using their wealth to signal their allyship with non-whites. Moreover, wealthier whites receive the greatest advantage of still operational vestiges of the old norms that privilege whiteness. One may note here the extent to which vilification of whites in popular culture tends to focus more vitriolically on the poor and uneducated, such as the archetypal 'redneck' or 'white trash'.

This problem results in part from a simplistic and dyadic understanding of the old status quo. The discourse around white privilege (including from white identitarians) takes the former situation of unchallenged white supremacy to imply that whites in general experienced untrammelled enjoyment. That is to say, it notes the exclusion of non-whites by the norm of whiteness and infers wrongly from this that whites enjoyed simple inclusion by dint of their whiteness. This view, I think, conflates sufficient and necessary conditions: historically, in some parts of the world, it has been *necessary*, if one wanted to be part of the most privileged elite group, to be white, which for our purposes relates to the fact that being white has been a powerful norm

Difference

in Western societies. This relegates everyone who is non-white to the category of the abnormal. Being white has never been a *sufficient* basis for being a member of any kind of elite group, however, in part because there are all kinds of other norms on the basis of which most white people have been deemed abnormal, and also because no white person was ever quite white enough to meet the norm to which they were held. Rather, poor whites, in particular, were under constant suspicion of being of mixed race or degenerate, for example, and so were themselves racially suspect within an overtly racist white supremacist society.

Differential Abnormalization

There is reason to believe that the abnormalization of whiteness I have just described is *sui generis* in relation to race, rather than being the general pattern of the operation of the norm of diversity. Other indices of diversity do not show the same effects, partly perhaps because the sheer existence of whiteness is so ephemeral. After all, racial categories are biologically dubious ones that might be expected to disappear, and even insofar as there is such a thing as a white race, its disappearance as a result of miscegenation could occur without any harm identifiable by currently prevailing norms. So to say it is not OK to be white might be said to be a function of the fact that the normative future is one where white people simply do not exist either as a conceptual category or as a phenotype. By contrast, consider the analogous statements, 'it's OK to be male', 'it's OK to be straight' – or even, 'it's OK to be cis'. I am speaking purely hypothetically, but it seems to me that saying maleness is OK is likely to get some pushback, but

Difference

not, I think, to the same extent as saying it is OK to be white. One reason for this might be that feminism has vilified masculinity less than critical race discourse has vilified whiteness. And while masculinity, particularly its 'toxic' variant, might today be considered inimical to some degree, and even biological maleness might be suspect, male *gender identity* is normalized by dint of the normalization of transmen qua men, if nothing else. I think the claim that 'it's OK to be straight' would not really draw much complaint. Indeed, there are attempts to go rather further than such a statement, viz. to stage 'straight pride' parades in contradistinction to 'gay pride' parades. These have certainly drawn criticism, but nowhere near to the same extent as 'white pride' advocacy has. Stating 'it's OK to be cis' at this point I think would barely make sense to people, since we are clearly less advanced in the normalization of being transgender, such that there is not really any question mark over the normality of being cis.

I suspect that the differentiation here might also reflect the fact that, for whatever reason, in the discourse, race has come to trump gender or sexuality. Note the derisiveness with which 'white feminism' and 'white women' have come to be spoken of. Femaleness in the current year is not enough to exculpate whiteness. By comparison, there is no specific attack on 'black masculinity', which would say, OK these guys are black, but they're still *male*, in the way that, rhetorically, this approach works to discredit feminists on the basis that, OK, they are women, but they're still *white*. This, I suspect, has much to do with the power dynamics in these cases. In the case of the relationship between whites and non-whites, in particular between whites and blacks, there is a history of extreme power relations (slavery, lynching). Women can point to a history of

Difference

frequently lethal, often sexual, violence by men against them, but the prevalent thought is that white women benefited from the enslavement of black men in a way that black men have never benefited from the subjugation of white women by white men.

The normative hierarchy between these categories tracks the extent to which race operates much more than gender, and to which gender in turn trumps sexuality, in contemporary America in particular, as indicators of inequality. To cite some basic, raw data that illustrates this, in 2017 the median income for men in the United States was almost 25 per cent more than that for women (an all-time low gap), while the median income for white men was almost 45 per cent more than that for black men, with the gap between the two widening, if anything (the disparity between black and white women was much less, but still somewhat higher than the gap between white men and white women).[4] Sexuality, by contrast, is not included as a factor in the same datasets, but whereas gay men historically earned between 5 and 10 per cent less than straight men, recent research finds that this gap has been inverted and gay men now earn 10 per cent more than their straight counterparts;[5] among women, lesbians have, for a long time, tended to have higher incomes than straight women.[6]

I do not mean to reduce questions of discrimination or oppression to crude economic quantification. However, I do believe this data indicates that not all discrimination or oppression is equal, even if it all does intersect. It indicates that being black in America today may be a greater economic disadvantage than being female, which may in turn be a greater economic disadvantage than being gay. I am suggesting that, in the effort to overcome this disadvantage, it is justified

Difference

to emphasize non-whiteness or blackness more than femaleness or a fortiori non-heterosexuality as an index of diversity.

There are likely additional reasons for this difference in emphasis, of course. One might be the essential invisibility and indeterminability of sexuality. Given that gender is increasingly no longer considered to be determinable by visible cues, race has become perhaps the most visible of these categories, hence the index by which diversity can be most immediately gauged. At the other end of the spectrum, the fluidity of sexual categories means that the difference between heterosexuals and LGBT people has always been less clear than that between the genders or races – even though these too have never been absolutely manifest. Thus, while this was hardly a perfect solution, gay people have always had a greater potential to avoid discrimination by effecting not to be gay, an option of 'passing' that is much less viable for most black people and women.

Lastly, we should logically presume that, since the norm of diversity derives its impetus from opposing the previously reigning norms, then, if it emphasizes race above all else, this would seem to imply that race was the most previously normalized category too, which is to say, that whiteness is today being vilified proportionally to the extent it was previously valorized. This observation might make the new norm seem just, but there is little to indicate that it is generating justice.

Justice

The path of tendential abnormalization of whiteness that has been pursued as a solution to racial injustice is problematic on my view precisely because it aims to combat one norm with another. By contrast, the fight for the liberation of sexuality seems to have had extraordinary success without any such major counter-normalization. Rather, it seems to have achieved its success simply by bestowing equal validation upon every sexuality.

An attempt to extend the paradigm of equal validation more broadly emerged early in the 2010s, particularly online (and most specifically on the blogging site Tumblr), reusing an older rubric of 'social justice'. This amounted more or less to the demand that everyone be deemed normal, specifically by demanding that positive norms be made so elastic that they could accommodate everyone. In relation to sexual activity, as discussed above, the old sexual norm of married heterosexuality was cast aside in favour of a norm of consent, such that sexual activity or the absence thereof is understood to be normal as long as there is no problem of consent among any of the parties involved, but allows everything else. Within ultra-progressive online (and indeed offline) communities, any suggestion that anything within this domain of consensual sex might be taboo has come to be vilified as 'kink-shaming' – that is, it is now forbidden to forbid in relation to consensual sex. Attitudes towards nonconsensual sex in this milieu is similarly hyperbolic and unforgiving, with the slogan 'kill all rapists' enjoying considerable popularity.

Attempts to apply a consistently permissive new norm that would validate everyone equally in other areas have been less successful, however – precisely, I think, because of the absence of an abnormal rump to vilify analogously to the way rapists and paedophiles provide a clear set of abnormals to vilify in relation to sex. The norm of 'beauty' is one example. There is no basis for judging beauty (understood as making a

Difference

judgement about human aesthetics) that is not nakedly prejudicial. It has been explicitly demanded on social media that all women be deemed 'beautiful'. This demand peaked and was then discredited on social media in the course of the 2010s, leaving millions of Google results for the exact phrase 'all women are beautiful' in its wake. The problem with this slogan is that it renders 'beauty' analytically indistinguishable from 'femaleness' and thus makes any statement that some *particular* woman is beautiful meaningless. A demand that all cases be found normal and that abnormality be abolished ends up amounting to a demand for the abolition of any norm in a given area. Insisting that all women are beautiful amounts to saying that no women are beautiful, or that there is no such thing as beauty. However, it is no accident that there was no explicit demand that we 'abolish beauty'. There was general awareness that being judged 'beautiful' has immense recognitive import for women – that is, they derive a feeling of self-worth and validation by being deemed 'beautiful', and a corresponding feeling of depredation when they are deemed 'ugly'. This indeed is why the demand was restricted to women, rather than demanding that all *people* be recognized as beautiful. The fact that I restrict the significance of this norm specifically to women is not to imply that men are immune to concern about their appearance, only that there are different specific norms in relation to men. Since abolishing beauty would rob all women of this recognition, the demand was made not to destroy but to extend it. But if this had been successful, it would surely have the same effect as abolishing the notion – what recognition can I derive from a completely automatic and trivial judgement of beauty? At most, perhaps, that women are beautiful, *unlike men*.

Difference

That said, there is a way in which this demand that all women be acknowledged as beautiful has been implemented that preserves the discrimination that makes judgements of beauty meaningful, which is to say a way in which the demand has been formally followed while actually changing nothing much in practice. We see this trivial recognition in the way in which women's selfies are routinely applauded online by their audience. That is, to put it bluntly, that women's female friends in particular generally tell them that they are beautiful in any picture they post online. Given how automatic the plaudits are, I would suggest that they are essentially meaningless, and that the intensity of the reaction, particularly the number of 'likes', stands as a proxy for a positive reaction. The mere presence of an explicitly positive reaction that is insufficiently enthusiastic might be taken for faint praise that damns. And the basic situation here in relation to the norm of beauty remains the same: no amount of praise, no number of likes, will ever be enough, since there is no upper limit, no assurance of complete and final beautifulness.

The tactic of telling all women they are beautiful was an attempt to make a norm just. The general problem with this is that norms cannot be just – they function, rather, by holding everyone to be inadequate, albeit it never equally so. They will always to some degree be unfair to everyone, and always more unfair to some than to others.

More charitably, one might say that the social justice agenda does in effect demand the abolition of norms, even if not explicitly, by pushing them to their limit. There is no indication that it has had or will have this effect, however. The problem here with the social justice strategy is, on the contrary, its sheer normativity: it may not counterpose a norm of what counts as beautiful

Difference

to the existing norm, but it does depend on a norm of conduct in which everyone is treated fairly in society. The problem with its normativity – which is indeed a problem with normativity in general – is that it takes up the abstract demand for fairness without attending to the effects such demands have, which is not simply to bring about fairness but, rather, to complicate things still further.

Of course, this demand for equality and justice is not a novel one. What we see here is a conflict of the norm of equality with the norms of individualism. To an extent, the norm of equality is presumed by contemporary liberal individualism, which takes all people to be equal in their individuality. However, in relation to almost any other norm, individuals are palpably unequal and indeed may become even less equal as they competitively pursue that norm. Thus, the individualist pursuit of norms contradicts the norm of equality. Yet, there remains a pervasive desire to make them function together, as with the norms of health and pleasure. Clearly, there is a division today between those, broadly on the political left, who emphasize equality and those, broadly on the political right, who emphasize individuality, but ultimately neither side is willing to completely abnegate either norm, nor does either side represent a solution to the contradiction between them. While one might point to societies in which individuality is denigrated in the name of equality, in the West, leftists are in certain respects the greatest advocates of individuality. Of course, such leftists maintain that there is no inherent contradiction between individuality and equality, but I simply disagree. Even if individuality is in a supposedly apolitical or non-economic sphere, such as fashion, the palpable difference between individuals' ability

Difference

to approximate the norm will make them palpably unequal.

It is not so much the principles at stake here that are the problem, but their transformation into norms. Individuality might be a virtue, but treating it as a norm is pernicious and even self-contradictory inasmuch as it means making it compulsory to be maximally individual. Equality similarly might be an important legal or ethical principle, but the absolutization of equality by turning it into a norm makes it dangerous. Relatedly, the elevation of difference into an absolute norm is an impediment to any attempt to produce commonality (or a fortiori universality), which is also a serious issue: any social activity or formation presupposes the identification both of differences and commonalities between people. The effective aim of contemporary efforts in the name of social justice is to get all applicable norms to work harmoniously together qua norms, which seems both obvious and laudable, but I would suggest is clearly impossible to achieve, or even meaningfully to approximate. There is a particular problem with the core nexus of the norms of equality and difference. There is no inherent tension between the *principles* of difference and equality, inasmuch as we can simply and truthfully state that we are all different from one another but equal in our humanity, but once these principles become norms, they are absolutized to the point of contradiction.

Conclusion

There are two obvious radical conclusions – one broadly right wing, the other left wing – that one might draw from the claims in this book. I will not draw either myself, but will outline them.

One could, on the one hand, come to the conservative conclusion that we need a return to tradition, to rules, to escape the tyranny of norms by going back to the status quo ante. Such a reactionary response is not only in relation to norms, but is, rather, a general attitude to the vicissitudes of the contemporary situation, and is seen in all forms of conservatism. A specifically anti-norm form would have to be a relatively radical one, however. If it were to heed what I have said in this book, it would have to enjoin us to return to pre-late modern life. Such political stances are today readily encounterable online in the form of varying degrees of primitivism, and medievalist fantasies of returns to forms of monarchism, theocracy and/or feudalism. The problem with all such fantasies from the perspective of this book is that they all at least threaten to be normative themselves. That is, for all the 'trad' posturing of neo-reactionaries, we can only ever understand the past through the lens of our

Conclusion

current culture, based on partial evidence that has come down to us, and consequently we inevitably misunderstand it. Any revival of past forms will evidently be in some respects different from the original, and the danger in relation to norms is that what was an organic mode of society or government in the past becomes a norm in the attempt to revive it, leading to something very different. While one might say one wants genuinely to return to the past, to wipe out all vestiges of modernity, it is simply not clear how one could possibly do this. Even the most apocalyptic scenario for the destruction of contemporary civilization would not in fact destroy all vestiges of our contemporary culture. Simply to go back is impossible: whatever might happen next, whatever we try to do, we cannot just wipe away our involvement with norms and return to a world without them, unmarked by the experience.

A more minimal conservative project would be to reassert the model of the rule against that of the norm. However, it is not at all clear that a society of the rule would be more desirable overall than a society of the norm. Certainly, when we look at the opening descriptions of Foucault's *Discipline and Punish*, it is not obvious that a society in which we hang, draw and quarter regicides is preferable to one in which we incarcerate people, even if the converse is not at all obvious either. The bottom line when considering the future of our society must be that we simply don't know what the implications of moving to a society of the rule from a society of the norm would actually be, thus we have scant motivation to pursue such a shift, even to the extent that we could deliberately engineer it, which is itself I think quite a dubious prospect. And even if we did know and could engineer the change, we would surely be overwhelmingly likely to be influenced

Conclusion

by our contemporary norms in our estimation of what was desirable, hence fulfilling rather than breaking with them by pursuing such a course.

On the other hand, there is a liberal-progressive response that sees a solution in moving beyond norms to a greater freedom which builds on the momentum of the rejection of the old norms of the twentieth century to reject all norms whatsoever – a position that Foucault effectively champions in the first volume of his *History of Sexuality*, albeit only specifically in relation to sex. This is a more realistic approach than the reactionary one inasmuch as it is only a negative vision, thus does not rely on anything specific being achieved in practice. But the simplicity of this negativity will be difficult to achieve. Surely it is more likely that norms will mutate before they are dispensed with, and indeed in strange way. In effect, this is what we have already seen with the emergence of our new norms: the form of the norm has colonized and suborned the challenge to the old norms, and became stronger and more malleable for it. Moreover, the fact that we don't know if what will come will be better or worse also bedevils a purely negative project too.[1] Lastly, even negation itself can become normative, which is something I think we have seen in the historical implementation of Marxism.[2]

Strictly speaking, I do not believe either of these positions, right or left, can be inferred from this present study. Rather, they constitute possible *responses* to it. I do not think either is very realistic, however. Indeed, I am tempted to suggest that they are ways of coping with our predicament through a fantasy of escape rather than serious challenges to our norms.

What then are we to do, as individuals caught in the normative warp? Are we simply trapped? Modestly, as individuals, we must respond in some way to our

Conclusion

predicament – navigate it, as it were. I have certainly responded to my own situation at a personal level, but I do not believe this response comes straightforwardly from the insights I've shared here, so think it would be inappropriate to present this as a conclusion. I think what can schematically be said is that some form of cognitive support is needed if we are not to fall nihilistically into the gyre of norms. That is to say, it is easy enough to enjoin people to resist norms. We can say that one should stop aiming at perfection, stop holding both oneself and others to such high normative standards, stop propounding visions of a perfected future. But there is a serious psychological need that all this perfectionism serves, even if it is a form of self-torture for the most part, namely what to aim for in life. Without the norm, the modern hedonistic individual is thrown back only on their immediate desires, no longer normativized but simply immanent. Such immanentism is seemingly advocated both by Deleuze in his emphasis on desire and by Foucault in his emphasis on a return to 'bodies and pleasures'.[3] The immanence of affects and impulses might indeed be, as Foucault puts it, a *point d'appui* (rallying point) for a counterattack against norms, but that counterattack would need materiel to match the armaments of its opponent, which means not merely a certain conceptual vocabulary, but an entire cultural form. Personally, I tend to agree with Lacan, that the only repository of sufficient resources here is likely to be religion,[4] even if I can hardly rule out other possible bases for the counterattack, and even though a pivot towards religion must look alarmingly like a simple reactionary move to restore the status quo ante norms.

While we desperately need a way to personally orient ourselves, something to cling to against the ever-increasing suction of absolute normativity, large-scale

Conclusion

social and political change must occur if we are to forge a way out of the society of the norm. I do not believe, for reasons I have outlined in other work, that such complex questions can be usefully addressed through individualized advice. For all that the personal may be political, individual actions do not predictably scale up to political solutions: the advice to 'be the change you want to see in the world' is not a serious political strategy.

This difficulty indeed applies even to supposedly political solutions to social problems. That is to say that the complexity of the social means that even thought-out, evidence-based solutions might not work in practice, given the indefinitely large number of relevant variables that apply in the real world. And when we are talking about defeating or replacing norms as a social ordering, we cannot seriously claim to be able to think through or have evidence applicable to such a global, revolutionary change. Indeed, I do not believe it is possible to know in advance that getting rid of norms is going to be desirable.

That said, for all that what replaces norms might, in any number of senses, be worse, it nonetheless seems to me that there is something like an objective necessity to supersede norms. One reason for this is the impetus that comes from our unbearable personal anxiety dealing with them. Another is more global: the norm as a social phenomenon is implicated in all our contemporary crises. In particular, I believe that norms are one factor in the existential crisis represented by the destruction of the natural environment: our quest for perfection is driving much of our destruction of the ecosphere because it cannot be satisfied. That said, I think there are enough drivers for this destruction that ending this quest would do little to curtail it by itself, although

Conclusion

conversely it seems hard to see how a society of norms will not destroy the environment unless environmental protection is adopted as a fundamental norm that restrains all the others.

Why can't we simply abandon norms? It is certainly easier to say than to do. It is something I have tried to do in my political thought, but this has required a constant effort: in our society, we gravitate towards the default of having a norm, even if the particular norm we have may vary. This poses an acute difficulty for any attempt to address the problem posed by norms politically, inasmuch as such political efforts themselves gravitate towards a normative form. This tendency is evident across a broad spectrum, from high academic political theory to popular political movements. At the former end, I have dealt elsewhere with the almost ineluctable tendency towards normativity in political philosophy in particular.[5] The temptation to think that our vision for improving society is the only correct one and that all others are wrong and, worse, enemies of the good is incredibly hard not to fall into. As I have argued elsewhere, the only prophylactic I can conceive against this is a constant and difficult self-discipline against normative thinking, which is much more achievable in print than it is in everyday habits of thought.

At the other end of the spectrum, I would note the contemporary tendency in popular politics towards conspiracy theories (a tendency which, in my view, is increasingly visible on the left in addition to its more longstanding stronghold on the right). Conspiracy theories are fuelled by, among other things, the premise that everyone ought to be and feel perfectly fine, and the idea that something must be terribly wrong if people are sick or unhappy. This is a popular modern premise, basically Manichean, and indeed I think it

Conclusion

can be seen much more widely in our personal lives: if something goes wrong, we think someone must be to blame, whether it is another individual, a person in authority or a system. We not only strive for perfection but normatively believe that everything is supposed to work perfectly, and any absence of perfection has the potential to enrage us. If we cannot identify a responsible agency, we must invent agents against whom to rage.

Increasingly, we have a politics of mutually opposed outrage. Outrage is what happens when people understand the world to work a certain way and it turns out not to do so.[6] This is perhaps not unique to the age of the norm, but, like many things, is greatly accentuated by it. In a particular contemporary lexicon, the word 'problematic' has come to be the standard term of condemnation, which I think reveals the extent to which we now find ourselves in an era of unprecedented intolerance of everything. Everything, after all, has some flaw, some problem with it. If pointing this out in and of itself is a condemnation of its very being, as it now seems to be, we are quite literally beyond redemption.

Still, we can surely hope that the age of the norm will either end or at least undergo further serious mutation. By the time I was a child, in the 1980s, the term 'square' had migrated from being a countercultural insult against members of the dominant culture to a demotic insult thrown at youngsters who were deemed to be too serious for the new dominant culture. To some extent I think this reflects a kind of uprising of popular sentiments that were never really in line with the old norms against them, using a new vocabulary. Isn't the new notion of the 'normie' something like turning back against the new normal in the same way people rebelled against the old normal 'squares'? The normie and the

Conclusion

bugman are perhaps to the contemporary situation what the square was two generations ago.

However, what we see in the new norms is the extraordinary inventiveness of the norm qua a peculiar instantiation of power to adapt and incorporate resistance to it. Yet, as Foucault would have it, power will always meet resistance and the new norm is no exception. What remains less clear is what shape such resistance can coherently take, and to what extent it too can be normatively repurposed and colonized. And we can be sure, moreover, that even if we do dispense with norms, we will nevertheless always be imbricated within some strategy of power. With this in mind, perhaps the point is not to change the world, given the radical unpredictability of the outcome, but rather to critique it, on the basis that awareness is the best aid we can have to navigating the vicissitudes of history, and that interpretation is not something to which our situation is simply indifferent.

Notes

Preface
1 In making this claim, I am influenced by Stéphane Legrand's reading of Foucault's work on norms, although in point of fact I reject what he says as an interpretation of Foucault. Stéphane Legrand, *Les Normes chez Foucault*. Paris: Presses Universitaires de France, 2007. For my position, see Mark G. E. Kelly, 'What's in a Norm? Foucault's Conceptualisation and Genealogy of the Norm', *Foucault Studies*, 27, 2019.

Chapter 1: Genealogy
1 Christopher Lasch, *The Culture of Narcissism*. New York: Norton, 1979.
2 Luc Boltanski and Eve Chiapello, *The New Spirit of Capitalism*. London: Verso, 2017.
3 So, for example, Ian Hacking might be right that our conceptions of the normal are linked by being part of the historical shift from determinism to indeterminism that he diagnoses, but this connection is quite beyond the scope of the current book. See Ian Hacking, *The Taming of Chance*. Cambridge: Cambridge University Press, 1990, p. 179.

4 My close analytical work to derive this definition can be found in Kelly, 'What's in a Norm? Foucault's Conceptualization and Genealogy of the Norm', *Foucault Studies*, 27/27 (2019): 1–22.
5 Georges Canguilhem, *The Normal and the Pathological* [1966]. Dordrecht: D. Reidel, 1978.
6 There are other accounts of the origin of norms that portray it as coming precisely out of statistics, but I would simply maintain that these accounts are mistaken. Perhaps the most prominent such account is Hacking's *The Taming of Chance*. Hacking, however, is apt to portray things in this way precisely because he is doing the history of statistics, not the history of norms, and he is therefore not looking for a non-statistical origin of the concept of the norm.
7 Hacking, *The Taming of Chance*, p. 178.
8 The *Oxford English Dictionary* (*OED*) notes an isolated use of the word as early as 1598, but in its modern sense only in a zoological journal from 1825 – and does not record its use in relation to human beings until 1886, unsurprisingly in a medical publication. Google's 'Books Ngram Viewer' indicates that usage of the word 'normal' in books in English began after 1820 and rose continuously, with an exponential explosion in the early twentieth century to an early peak in 1920. The *OED* records 'norm' first in 1821, but the notion of a social norm only in 1900. Google's Ngram Viewer shows use of the word 'norm' beginning to grow in usage in the mid-nineteenth century and growing almost every year since, something that is also true of the much more recently coined term 'normative'; the word 'normal' still appears at ten times the frequency of the word 'norm', though the gap is narrowing. By contrast, for the French cognates, *normal* and *norme*, the gap is closer to a factor of two for *normal* over *norme*.
9 Canguilhem, *The Normal and the Pathological*, p. 150.

10 Michel Foucault, *Discipline and Punish* [1975]. London: Penguin, 1977, pp. 195ff. Michel Foucault, *Abnormal* [1999]. London: Verso, 2003, pp. 43ff.
11 Foucault, *Discipline and Punish*, p. 184.
12 Foucault in *Discipline and Punish* sees modern disciplinary power precisely as producing a 'modern soul'.
13 Michel Foucault, *Security, Territory, Population* [2004]. Basingstoke: Palgrave Macmillan, 2007, p. 58. This passage seems clear enough to me, but is complicated immediately afterwards by a comment of Foucault's proposing effectively to redesignate what he has just called 'normalization' neologistically as 'normation', and instead use the term 'normalization' to refer to statistics-based norms. Some commentators (in particular, Mary Beth Mader, *Sleights of Reason. Norm, Bisexuality, Development*. Albany: State University of New York Press, 2011) have seized on this to assert that for Foucault normalization is in general a statistical phenomenon. Foucault, however, only ever mentions 'normation' in this one passing remark, and he is entirely clear that non-statistical 'normation' is what he elsewhere consistently calls 'normalization'. For my full reading and treatment of alternative readings of Foucault on this point, see Kelly, 'What's in a Norm?', pp. 10–13.
14 Sigmund Freud criticized the very Christian ethical commandment to love one's neighbour as being impossibly unrealistic. What Freud fails to recognize is that this commandment was always tempered by the realization that it was precisely not possible to achieve – rather, it was intended as something to aim for, and a basis on which to atone for one's trespasses against others. That Freud viewed it as he did I think is indicative of the age of the norm he was already living in a hundred years ago. See Sigmund Freud, *Civilization and Its Discontents*. New York: W. W. Norton, 1961.

15 My concept of the meta-norm perhaps resembles Hans Kelsen's concept of a *Grundnorm*, but Kelsen is not an influence on me and I will not explore this comparison here.
16 For a study that focuses on closely related matters in a French context, see Boltanski and Chiapello, *The New Spirit of Capitalism*.
17 To give a singular concrete example, changes in attitudes to sexual behaviour, which I deal with here, can be seen in the United States to pertain to whites vastly more than to black Americans. See J. M. Twenge, R. A. Sherman and B. E. Wells, 'Changes in American Adults' Sexual Behavior and Attitudes, 1972–2012', *Archives of Sexual Behavior*, 44 (2015): 2273–2285, 2281.

Chapter 2: New Norms

1 Adam Bear and Joshua Knobe, 'Normality: Part Descriptive, Part Prescriptive', *Cognition*, 167 (2017): 25–37.
2 I was tempted to say that we can see this reaction palpably in those from that era who still survive, but given that they have lived through the normative changes that have since occurred, their position is rather more ambiguous than that: even when they express horror at contemporary life, we must suspect that it is not the raw horror of a person from the past, but one coming from a contemporary conservative normative perspective.
3 By 'existentialism', I am referring primarily to Jean-Paul Sartre's thought, most particularly in his *Being and Nothingness* [1943]. London: Routledge, 1983. On existentialism in general, see David E. Cooper, *Existentialism: A Reconstruction*. Oxford: Wiley-Blackwell, 1999.
4 My argument in relation to difference is directly drawn from that made by Alain Badiou, in particular from his *Ethics*. London: Verso, 2001.

5 Strictly speaking, the Augustinian notion of 'original sin' is not strictly necessary to recognize man's sinful nature: in Eastern Christianity, in particular, the inevitability and ubiquity of sin is recognized without qualifying it as 'original'. Indeed, one might suggest that the stringency of the Western, Augustinian notion of original sin has precisely contributed to its unravelling.
6 Foucault, 'Theatrum Philosophicum', *Critique*, 282: 885.
7 *Eudaimon*. In his *Nicomachean Ethics*, Book I, Chapter 10, Aristotle suggests that happiness is precisely what girds us against the influence of fortune, although he (as always) takes the *via media* position that extreme ill-fortune might still destroy happiness. Aristotle is, of course, given his antiquity, not a normative thinker in the sense I am discussing here.
8 I will note here the extent to which radical French thinkers in the late twentieth century tried to break open this complex – presumably in their context before it had fully solidified. Foucault famously, in the first volume of his *History of Sexuality*, distinguished pleasure from desire, suggesting that ruse of the former against the latter to resist the '*dispositif* of sex'. See Michel Foucault, *The History of Sexuality, Vol. I*. London: Penguin, 1978. I think Foucault's stratagem, at least at this point, offers us approximately nothing inasmuch as our desire is now based around pleasure anyway, perhaps in part as a result of his intervention. Gilles Deleuze and Jacques Lacan took the opposite approach, opposing pleasure on the basis of lauding desire. With them we might at least say, 'Another desire is possible', given that, in a non-hedonistic context, desire might be determined as something other than following base inclinations.
9 Ludwig Feuerbach, *The Essence of Christianity*. New York: Harper Torchbooks, 1957.
10 W. E. B. du Bois noted already in the mid-twentieth century

that 'The ideal of every American is the millionaire', at a time when having a million dollars was still actually synonymous with great wealth. To the extent that this is true, it implies the shift I am diagnosing was in train well before I am positing it. At the very least, I admit that, at the leading edge in America, the normalization of wealth was certainly palpable by this point. See *The Autobiography of W. E. B. Du Bois*. Oxford: Oxford University Press, 2007.

11 Hans Pongratz and Guenter Voss, 'From Employee to "Entreployee": Towards a "Self-Entrepreneurial" Work Force?', *Concepts and Transformation*, 8 (2003): 239–254.

12 Or more precisely, as found in the experience of shifting from collective to individualized bargaining in Australian workplaces during the first decade of this century, the individualization of wage negotiation delivered a net benefit to workers who were highly skilled, thus in high demand, but tended to drive down the wages of the more numerous, lower-skilled workers, although this tendency was sometimes adumbrated by the continuing presence of powerful labour unions whose influence tended to inflate the bargaining power of individual workers in the relevant sectors. See David Peetz and Alison Preston, 'Individual Contracting, Collective Bargaining and Wages in Australia', *Industrial Relations Journal*, 40 (2009): 444–461.

13 Luc Boltanski and Eve Chiapello, 'The New Spirit of Capitalism', *International Journal of Politics, Culture and Society*, 18 (2005): 161–188.

14 It is worth noting that between 2007 and 2014 there were small shifts in all Christian groups surveyed (not counting Jehovah's Witnesses, whose average position remained stable) towards accepting homosexuality, recorded by the Pew *Religious Landscape Survey*. However,

the basic pattern within Protestantism of Evangelical opposition and mainline acceptance remained stable. See Pew Research Centre, 'Views About Homosexuality', *Religious Landscape Study*: https://www.pewforum.org/religious-landscape-study/views-about-homosexuality/; and 'US Religious Landscape Survey: Religious Beliefs and Practices', 1 June 2008: https://www.pewforum.org/2008/06/01/u-s-religious-landscape-survey-religious-beliefs-and-practices/.

15 The belief that God rewards Christians directly with material wealth does not yet seem to be a majority belief in the USA, although it does seem to have been growing strongly – however, even though it has attracted strong commentary, it has not apparently been systematically studied. In any case, I believe it is the very emergence of this tendency, rather than its absolute size, that is indicative.

16 Jacques Lacan, *On Feminine Sexuality: The Limits of Love and Knowledge*. New York: W. W. Norton, 1998, p. 3. Lacan says here that we are not forced to enjoy by anything, except by our superego, which is to say by our conscience, which incessantly tells us we should be enjoying ourselves. This description accords with the description I have provided of the operation of a norm of enjoyment. However, the concept of enjoyment, or more precisely *jouissance*, is a word of art of Lacan's that is normally left untranslated; it eludes easy definition. My position in relation to Lacan might be taken to be an historicization that makes what he thinks is a universal tendency into a recent development, but I think actually that what I am discussing is a specific determination of *jouissance* in our lifetime as a kind of easy pleasure, which is not at all how it has figured in other historical periods. Even if the general structure of *jouissance* means it is always superegotic, and other general features of it

identified by Lacan – its purely excessive character, its fundamental relation to sex, etc. – can be said to characterize *jouissance* across historical periods, there can also be a specific postconformist form of this, focused on individual gratification. If pleasure and satisfaction have always had some relation to *jouissance*, it does not follow that they have dominated it as fully as they do today. That said, the domination of *jouissance* by these things might well be said to reduce our capacity for actual enjoyment.

17 Although not widely recognized outside Australia, this is a local brand of a French multinational, Lactalis. It produces the leading flavoured milk brand in Australia, where upwards of 200 million litres of flavoured milk are sold per annum, close to ten litres of flavoured milk per person per year.

18 The Pew Research Center found in 2009 that approximately 50 per cent of Americans change religious affiliation at some point in their lives. See 'Faith in Flux': https://www.pewforum.org/2009/04/27/faith-in-flux/.

19 Angela Nagle, *Kill All Normies*. Winchester: Zero, 2017.

Chapter 3: Politics

1 Mark G. E. Kelly, 'Foucault and the Politics of Language Today', *Telos*, 191 (2020); and 'Is Fascism the Main Danger Today? Trump and Techno-Neoliberalism', *Telos*, 192 (2020).

2 Yascha Mounk, 'Americans Strongly Dislike PC Culture', *The Atlantic*, 10 October 2018.

3 'Poorly Educated Voters Hold the Keys to the White House: Daily Chart', *The Economist* (online), 11 November 2019.

Chapter 4: Sex

1 It has been claimed, however, that the term 'involuntary celibacy' was invented by a woman, and originally self-applied by a more gender-diverse community. See

Peter Baker, 'The Woman Who Accidentally Started the Incel Movement', *Elle*, 1 March 2016: https://www.elle.com/culture/news/a34512/woman-who-started-incel-movement/. Thanks to Robert Carson for pointing me to this article.
2 For an extremely lengthy discussion of this view in early Christianity, see Michel Foucault, *Confessions of the Flesh*. London: Penguin, 2021.
3 Matthew 19:10–12; Corinthians 7:8–9. The Catholic Catechism indeed takes a rather more pro-chastity line though than either Jesus or even Paul, inveighing that 'All the baptized are called to chastity' (2348).
4 *Catechism of the Catholic Church*, 2358–9.
5 Jacques Lacan, 'Kant with Sade', *October*, 51 (1989): 55–75.
6 The Australian advocacy organization, People with Disability Australia, is currently lobbying the government to subsidize sexual services to the disabled. See https://pwd.org.au/sex-work-and-the-ndis-frequently-asked-questions/.
7 J. M. Twenge, R. A. Sherman and B. E. Wells, 'Changes in American Adults' Sexual Behavior and Attitudes, 1972–2012', *Archives of Sexual Behavior*, 44 (2015): 2273–2285, 2278.
8 Katie Way, 'I Went on a Date with Aziz Ansari. It Turned into the Worst Night of my Life', *babe*, 13 January 2018: https://babe.net/2018/01/13/aziz-ansari-28355
9 Catharine A. MacKinnon, 'Feminism, Marxism, Method, and the State: Toward Feminist Jurisprudence', *Signs*, 8/4 (1983): 635–658.
10 There is perhaps here a point of contact with Eric Voegelin's expansive body of work on the Gnosticism of materialist modernity, but this has not influenced this book, and I will postpone reckoning with Voegelin's thought for the moment.

11 Kate Julian, 'Why Are Young People Having So Little Sex?', *The Atlantic*, December 2018: https://www.theatlantic.com/magazine/archive/2018/12/the-sex-recession/573949/.
12 Maurice Merleau-Ponty, *The Phenomenology of Perception*. London: Routledge, 2002, p. 194.
13 As I have pointed out elsewhere, the French concept of *sexe* actually has a somewhat broader definition than the English concept of 'sex', encompassing not only sexual intercourse and gender, but also the sexual organ. See Mark G. E. Kelly, *Foucault's History of Sexuality, Volume I* (Edinburgh University Press, 2013).
14 As has been widely noted, this logic actually seems to introduce an immanent contradiction into the phenomenon of being transgender: if there is no requirement for someone of a particular gender to present in any particular way, what is it that one can use to determine what their gender is? If gender is merely about a feeling with no connection to conventional femininity or masculinity, what does this feeling attach to? For this reason, the logic of the phenomenon of being transgender seems to point not merely towards gender fluidity, but towards the total dissolution of gender, at least from a normative standpoint, which would be its own self-supersession.
15 Ipsos, 'Global Attitudes Toward Transgender People', January 2018: https://www.ipsos.com/sites/default/files/ct/news/documents/2018-01/ipsos_report-transgender_global_data-2018.pdf.
16 Michel Foucault, *The Hermeneutics of the Subject*. New York: Palgrave Macmillan, 2005, pp. 17ff.
17 Jürgen Habermas, *The Theory of Communicative Action. Volume 1: Reason and the Rationalization of Society*. Boston: Beacon, 1984.

Chapter 5: Life

1 Foucault's clearest discussion of this concept is found in the final lecture of his *Society Must Be Defended*. New York: Picador, 2003.
2 Michel Foucault, *The Use of Pleasure: The History of Sexuality, Vol. II*. London: Penguin, 1985.
3 There is indeed a range of behaviours that we might read in this vein as, alternatively, an extreme adherence to a norm to the point that they constitute a form of resistance to the norm, even if this resistance is hardly effectual or relieving, and indeed might be deemed the worst possible response for the subject. I am thinking specifically of suicidal behaviours (in which category some cases of eating disorders, at least, do themselves belong) and the burgeoning disorders of the autism spectrum.
4 Suzanne Goldberg, 'Half of All US Food Produce Is Thrown Away, New Research Suggests', *Guardian*, 13 July 2016.
5 Of course, both these feasts also predate Christianity, and hence ultimately have nothing specifically Christian about them (except the name, in the case of Christmas). Moreover, this practice of fasting in relation to them has undergone a long decline within Western Christianity itself, not only as an effect of the secularization of the practices. The Advent fast was already declining considerably in Catholic practice during the Middle Ages (though it did not finally disappear until the twentieth century). However, the Catholic Lenten fast, until relatively recently, involved abstention from meat and animal products throughout the forty-day period, except on Sundays, two days of total fasting, and a week restricted to bread and water. Indults allowing people in different regions to eat any kind of food during most of Lent eroded these restrictions over the centuries, and by the twentieth century restrictions on eating during most of Lent completely disappeared for Western Rite Catholics.

In Protestantism, by contrast, although early Reformers did not radically forbid fasting, their shift of emphasis away from penitential practice made it optional and thus allowed it to disappear, with a similar ultimate result. In Eastern Christianity, by contrast, the fasting regimen remains notionally intact: for Orthodox Christians, close to 50 per cent of the year canonically involves some form of dietary restriction.

6 Jean-Paul Sartre, *The Wall*. Richmond: Calder, 2019.
7 David Pearce, 'The Abolitionist Project', 2007: https://www.hedweb.com/abolitionist-project/index.html.
8 The question of the relation of norms to fashion in general is one that I have decided to leave out of this book. I originally planned an extensive chapter on this question, but in the end I simply could not form a clear view of how fashion relates to norms. My provisional current view is that fashion is *sui generis*; it is surely influenced by norms, but it is ultimately a much older – if more superficial – phenomenon.

Chapter 6: Law

1 Michel Foucault, *The History of Sexuality, Vol. I*. London: Penguin, 1978, p. 144.
2 Gary Fields and John R. Emshwiller, 'Many Failed Efforts to Count Nation's Federal Criminal Laws', *The Wall Street Journal*, 23 July 2011.
3 Lyric R. Cabral, and David Felix Sutcliffe, dirs. *(T)error*. 2015.
4 Couch killed four people while driving under the influence and received a probationary sentence without gaol-time following his attorney's claim that he had diminished responsibility because his parents' wealth had caused him to lack boundaries. It is disputed to what extent this defence was actually responsible for lightening Couch's sentence. Some have pointed out

that those responsible even for fatal car crashes under the influence of alcohol frequently escape custodial sentences, indicating that the novel defence cannot be credited definitively when explaining the leniency on Couch. However, it seems to me that the number of fatalities and aggravating circumstances mean that Couch could not have ordinarily been expected to avoid being sent to prison.

5 Aja Romano, 'Why Everything is a Milkshake Duck', *Vox*, 25 March 2021: https://www.vox.com/culture/22350188/what-is-a-milkshake-duck-definition-explained-jensen-karp-cinnamon-toast-shrimp.

6 There's an important possible exception to this in the Eastern tradition, which rejects the Western Augustinian notion of original sin and instead enjoins believers to *theosis*, which is to say, to become God. This tradition clearly does enjoin believers to seek perfection. However, this tradition has no clear historical link to the notion of the norm, and can be differentiated from it strongly on the basis that there is no normative *expectation* of theosis, so much as only an animating *hope*. Salvation in the Eastern tradition certainly does not require a kind of complete theosis, moreover, or even its approximation.

7 Jacques Lacan, *The Ego in Freud's Theory and in the Technique of Psychoanalysis*. New York: Norton 1988, p. 128.

8 Sigmund Freud, 'The Loss of Reality in Neurosis and Psychosis' [1924], in *The Standard Edition of the Complete Psychological Works of Sigmund Freud*, trans. and ed. J. Strachey. New York: W. W. Norton. Freud, of course, also viewed religious belief as at least fairly close to delusion, but even he recognized significant differences between its tenability and that of psychosis *sensu stricto*.

9 Michel Foucault, *The History of Madness*. Abingdon: Routledge, 2006.

10 Fox Butterfield, 'Prisons replace hospitals for the nation's mentally ill', *New York Times*, 5 March 1998.
11 Seena Fazel and John Danesh, 'Serious Mental Disorder in 23,000 Prisoners: A Systematic Review of 62 Surveys', *The Lancet*, 9306 (2002): 545–550.
12 Thomas Curran and Andrew P. Hill, 'Perfectionism Is Increasing Over Time: A Meta-Analysis of Birth Cohort Differences from 1989 to 2016', *Psychological Bulletin*, 145/4 (2019): 410–429, 410.
13 Curran and Hill, 'Perfectionism Is Increasing Over Time', p. 420.
14 Bronze Age Pervert, *Bronze Age Mindset*. Independently published, 2018. The pseudonymous pervert reads back the aestheticization of the perfect body to the earliest traces of Western history, in a way that is implicitly, in my view, inter alia a way of providing a deep historical justification for contemporary work-out culture.

Chapter 7: Difference

1 For an extended discussion of the issues raised in this paragraph, see Mark G. E. Kelly, 'Discontinuity in Poststructuralist Epistemology: Foucault contra Deleuze and Derrida', *Cosmos and History*, 15/1 (2019).
2 NPR, 'Discrimination in America: Experiences and views of African Americans', Robert Wood Johnson Foundation, November 2017: https://legacy.npr.org/documents/2017/oct/discrimination-whites-final.pdf.
3 NPR, 'Discrimination in America', pp. 15ff.
4 US Department of Labor: https://www.dol.gov/agencies/wb/data/earnings.
5 Kitt Carpenter, 'Gay Men Used to Earn Less than Straight Men: Now They Earn More', *Harvard Business Review*, 4 December 2017: https://hbr.org/2017/12/gay-men-used-to-earn-less-than-straight-men-now-they-earn-more.
6 'Girl Power', *The Economist*, 13 February 2016: https://

www.economist.com/finance-and-economics/2016/02/13/girl-power.

Conclusion

1. I have tended in the past, following Foucault, to argue that this problem of the ambiguous outcome of a negative approach need not trouble us, and hence advocated that approach. At this point, however, I am inclined to take a more cautious line.
2. I deal with this normativity of Marxism, in both theory and practice, in detail in the first two chapters of Mark G. E. Kelly, *For Foucault: Against Normative Political Theory*. Albany: SUNY Press, 2018.
3. Michel Foucault, *The History of Sexuality, Vol. I*. London: Penguin, 1978, p. 157. There is much to be said about the difference between Deleuze and Foucault, and between desire and pleasure, and I intend to deal with this at length elsewhere. In this book, I have tended, *pace* Deleuze and Foucault, to treat desire and pleasure as almost synonymous. I will say at this point only that there is some possibility that Deleuze and Foucault are talking about almost exactly the same thing by using these two terms, as indicated by a remark Deleuze reports Foucault made to him, namely 'What I call pleasure is perhaps what you call desire'. See Gilles Deleuze, 'Desire and Pleasure', *Foucault and His Interlocutors*, ed. Arnold I. Davidson. Chicago: Chicago University Press, 1997, p. 189.
4. Jacques Lacan, *Triumph of Religion*. Cambridge: Polity, 2013, pp. 64–65.
5. Kelly, *For Foucault*; and 'Against Prophecy and Utopia: Foucault and the Future', *Thesis Eleven*, 120/1 (2014): 104–118.
6. As Lacan says, anger is 'when the little pegs no longer go into the little holes'. Jacques Lacan, *Anxiety: The Seminar of Jacques Lacan Book X*. Cambridge: Polity, 2004, p. 14.

Index

America, United States of x, 21, 25, 29, 42–6, 57–73, 81, 112, 131, 143, 155, 160
anxiety 25–6, 34, 48, 108–11, 114, 124, 155, 171
asexuality 82, 85
authenticity 30, 33, 42, 48, 79
average 1, 3–4, 22, 24–5, 55–6, 60, 65–7, 112, 116

beauty 111, 162–4
behaviour x, 8–10, 12, 20, 27–8, 32–33, 54–5, 57–61, 63, 66–7, 116, 130–2, 134, 138–43, 136, 148
biology 84, 90–1, 95, 97, 99–101, 106, 123, 158–9
bisexuality 77–8
body 8, 110–11, 118–19, 124–7, 137–8, 148, 170

Canguilhem, Georges 1–5, 10, 17, 100, 145
celibacy 76, 81–4
children 9–10, 25–6, 31–2, 39, 53–4, 79–82, 90, 95–6, 128–9
Christianity 12, 18, 33, 42–7, 83–4, 87, 92, 115, 135–7, 146
class, social 18, 39–40, 69–70
Coca-Cola 49–50
conformity 16–19
consent 79–81, 84–7, 88–92, 162
conservatism 44, 46–7, 62, 72–3, 167–8
conspiracy theories 172
COVID-19 x, 6, 120
critique 19–20, 22–3, 83, 86, 91, 148, 174

Deleuze, Gilles 33, 150, 170, 179
desire 13, 31, 35–8, 48–9, 75, 79–80, 82–4, 87–9, 91, 93, 101, 113, 116–18, 121, 136, 145, 170, 179, 189

education 9, 54, 68, 70

Index

enjoyment 35, 41, 47–51, 108, 112–13, 116–17, 120, 123, 157, 181–2
environment 171–2
essentialism 18, 30
ethics 10, 20, 35, 113
ethnicity 30, 51, 68, 152, 155
see also whiteness
etymology 1, 11
euthanasia 122–4
existentialism 29–30

family 25–6, 52–3, 90–1
fatness 116, 118–19
feminism 43, 83, 95–6, 159
food 66, 108–10, 112–15, 118–19, 121
Foucault, Michel 1–2, 5–6, 10–11, 17, 19, 22–3, 26, 28, 33, 90, 93–4, 105–6, 130, 143, 168–70, 174
Freud, Sigmund 49, 136–7

gender 18, 26, 39, 75–6, 78, 93–103, 127, 149, 159–61
God 12, 25, 135–6
grammar 5, 7
guilt 12, 98, 108, 133–5

happiness viii, 34–5, 37, 42, 54–5, 72, 110, 124,
health viii, 3, 10, 13–14, 67, 106–25, 128, 138–9, 142, 148
hedonism 18, 35–7, 42, 46–50, 58, 67, 73, 75, 107, 115, 117, 119, 123, 170
homosexuality 32, 76–7, 80–1, 84, 97–9
housework 96

identity 31, 35, 39, 47–8, 53, 75, 94, 96, 99–100, 102–5, 150–1, 156, 159
incel *see* celibacy
individualism 17–18, 28–31, 33, 35–7, 42–3, 46–8, 55–6, 72, 107, 117, 165
individuals 30–1, 34, 38, 51–2, 54, 82, 90, 99, 101, 103–4, 119, 150, 152–3, 165, 169

Lacan, Jacques 49, 136, 145, 170, 179, 181n.16
liberalism 17, 27, 35, 37, 43–4, 46, 62, 72, 85, 89, 91, 113, 165, 169

marriage 25, 44, 76, 79–82, 86, 88, 92, 94–5
masculinity 26, 30, 53, 84, 96, 159, 184
medicine 3–5, 7–9, 14, 66–7, 99–101, 106–7, 118–19, 121, 128, 137–45, 149
Middle Ages 6, 27, 185n.5
military 7–8
mind 8–9, 91, 126, 137–8, 140–1, 145
unconscious 20, 84, 98, 135, 140
monetization 38–9
monogamy 76, 79, 82, 87–9

naturalness 98–100, 113, 127–9
normalization 7, 9, 11, 32–3, 58–60, 79–81, 177n.13
normativity 4–5, 14, 16–20, 164–5, 170, 172
nutrition 109, 112, 115

191

Index

paedophilia 80–1, 162
philosophy 150–1, 172
plague 5–7
polyamory 88–9, 91
prison 9, 142–4
psychiatry 8–9, 133, 138, 142–4
psychoanalysis 101, 140, 145
 see also Freud, Sigmund; Lacan, Jacques
psychology viii, 9, 101, 133, 138–49, 155, 170

queerness 94

race 153, 158–61
 see also whiteness
rape 64, 80, 85, 160
religion 12, 27–8, 43–6, 48, 52–3, 115, 135–7, 170
 decline of 108
rules 1, 5, 7, 10–13, 131, 167–8

Sade, Marquis de 85
science 3–4, 24, 98–9, 107, 128
sex 10, 64, 75, 79–89, 92–4, 162
 see also gender

sex work 86
sexuality 10, 30–1, 43, 47, 75–90, 93–5, 97, 152–3, 160–2
sin 12, 128
sociology 1–2
statistics 4, 177n.13
subjectivity 4, 20–1, 101, 141, 145

tradition 36, 46–7, 73, 87–9, 115, 167
transgender 96–102, 149, 159
transhumanism 125
Trump, Donald x, 57–71, 73

universality ii, 25, 29–30, 51–3, 63–5

veganism 112–14
violence 32, 160

whiteness 21, 30–1, 152–61
women 26, 44, 53–4, 76, 85, 89, 95–6, 111, 152, 159–61, 163–4
work 39–42, 52–4
 see also housework; sex work